Walking the Lost Railways of Essex

David Gridley

Slowcoach Publishing
Canary Wharf, London

First published March 2010
Second edition September 2011

Copyright: David Gridley

All rights reserved. No reproduction permitted
without prior permission of the publisher.

Published by:
Slowcoach Publishing

Printed by:
Lavenham Press Ltd

Distributed by:
Swan Books, 27 Corbets Tey Road,
Upminster, Essex, RM14 2AR.

www.swanbooks.co.uk
e mail: slowcoach@me.com

ISBN:

978-0-9564128-0-5

Front and back cover artwork by Bill Newman

CONTENTS

Acknowledgements

This book could not have been written without the generous help and encouragement of a great number of people. In particular I would like to thank Jeremy Scott from Swan Books and Bill Byford of Lavenham Press for guiding this first time author through the minefields of book writing. I am also grateful to Simon Atkins for his advice on book layout and design as well as Bill Newman who managed to produced such a striking and retro looking front cover from my original ideas.

This book would be nothing without its photographs and for help with that I would like to thank all the staff at the Search Engine of the National Railway Museum (NRM) for their help in locating not only some vary rare photos but also the great selection of railway posters found in this book. Thanks also go to Beverley Cole, Marion Siskin, The Lens of Sutton Association, Brightlingsea Museum, Ashdon Museum and, of course, Ben for putting up with my endless trips to the countryside in search of the 21 walks in this book.

Finally, a big thank you to all of you for buying this book and walking the walks. I hope you enjoy them.

Disclaimer

The author does not accept responsibility for any inaccuracies that may appear in this book. While every attempt has been made to be as accurate as possible with each walk there may be occasions where, especially over time, details could change. For example, footpaths can be re-routed or the signage can be missing, pubs could close down or change name. At these times please exercise common sense and always undertake the walks with safety in mind.

Something Lost

This book is both a celebration and revelation of something lost. It is a celebration of the pioneering spirit and technological advances of the Victorian era that brought the railways to every corner of the UK. And it is a revelation because many people do not realise just how many branch lines have been lost, in the UK in general, and in Essex in particular, let alone where they ran to and why they closed. For the railways transformed our country. Today we see the function of the railway to mainly ferry commuters back and forth to work, whereas in the Victorian period it was very different. Whether it was new lines to the coast for seaside excursions, freight and goods to fuel the Industrial Revolution, commuter traffic into London, fresh produce to be delivered overnight on the milk trains, or the Light Railways built to give a lifeline to depressed rural areas. A new railway meant nothing short of a revolution to areas where the only way to get around was on foot, bicycle or horse and cart.

The growth of Essex was directly linked to the expansion of the railways and the eventual demise of many of the branch lines has left behind fascinating places to explore. You may have looked at an old bridge, stuck in the middle of nowhere, and wondered 'was there a railway here once?' Or maybe you have come across a disused station and felt your mind wander off to imagine life here all those years ago with steam trains clattering through. Well, this book will give you some answers. It will tell you where the lines ran, how they came to be there, and finally, why they closed down. All of that on guided circular walks that try to take in as many good pubs, stunning views and historic villages as I have been able to cram into the 21 walks in this book. If you were to look at a map of the railways around 1900 then, like most other counties, Essex would have a great deal more branch lines than it does today. In fact the county has lost 10 branch lines, 41 stations and close to 90 miles of track. The reason why these lines came and went tells us a lot about the growth of Essex.

In fact the story of any railway is also a story of the towns and villages that it touches and I have tried to create walks here that not only retrace disused lines and buildings, but also venture off to discover local landmarks and villages, to see how the railways affected the communities that they travelled through. In this way we can see what happens not only when a railway arrives in a new location, but also how things change when they disappear as well. I would be very happy if this book does nothing except put back another piece of our lost history by showing how the railways have affected and been affected by the areas that they run through. Only with this book in your hand will you be able to explore the long lost branch lines to the coast, the jam industry at Tiptree, The Gin and Toffee line to Thaxted and the steam railway that ended up being part of the London Tube network. All of these places deserve to be visited and through this book you can do just that.

Bradshaws Railway Map of 1907

Railways are undoubtedly great feats of both engineering and design; much of it quite beautiful. However once a decision is made, money found and a route decided, railways are built on only one thing – brute force. And it is precisely because of this huge physical effort that even today, some 40 or more years since some of the lines and stations in this book were torn up that evidence of them still remains, slicing through the landscape, leaving a lasting footprint if only we took the time to stop and look. That is what this book is really all about. I want you to travel to these places: walk the walks, linger in the villages, visit the pubs, and, of course, enjoy the railways. For there are unique stories here and many of them are part of the long-lost history of the county. For this book is also a tribute to Essex. This is a county of great contrasts where the urban sprawl of the south and east soon gives way to more peaceful rural areas where thatched roofs, country pubs and village greens seem too numerous to mention. There are villages and towns with such fascinating names as White Colne, Wickham Bishops, Stow Maries and Chipping Ongar. For you don't have to travel very far in Essex to find yourself in a remote and secluded area, possibly a place that was once touched by a long forgotten railway.

The stories of how and why the railways were built as well as why they disappeared tell you a lot about the history of Essex itself, and in the concluding chapter I have tried to bring together all these various thoughts into a picture of what the loss of these railways has meant to the county. Who knows, maybe the demise of the railways should not always be seen as a backward step?

So, you may be a walker who likes railways, a railway buff who likes to walk or perhaps you just picked up this guide in a bookshop because you were attracted to the title or the cover. Whatever the reason, it doesn't matter. What is really important is that you pick up this book, pull on your walking shoes and get exploring. When you do, I hope you will be able to find out as much about the hidden history of Essex as I have.

David Gridley

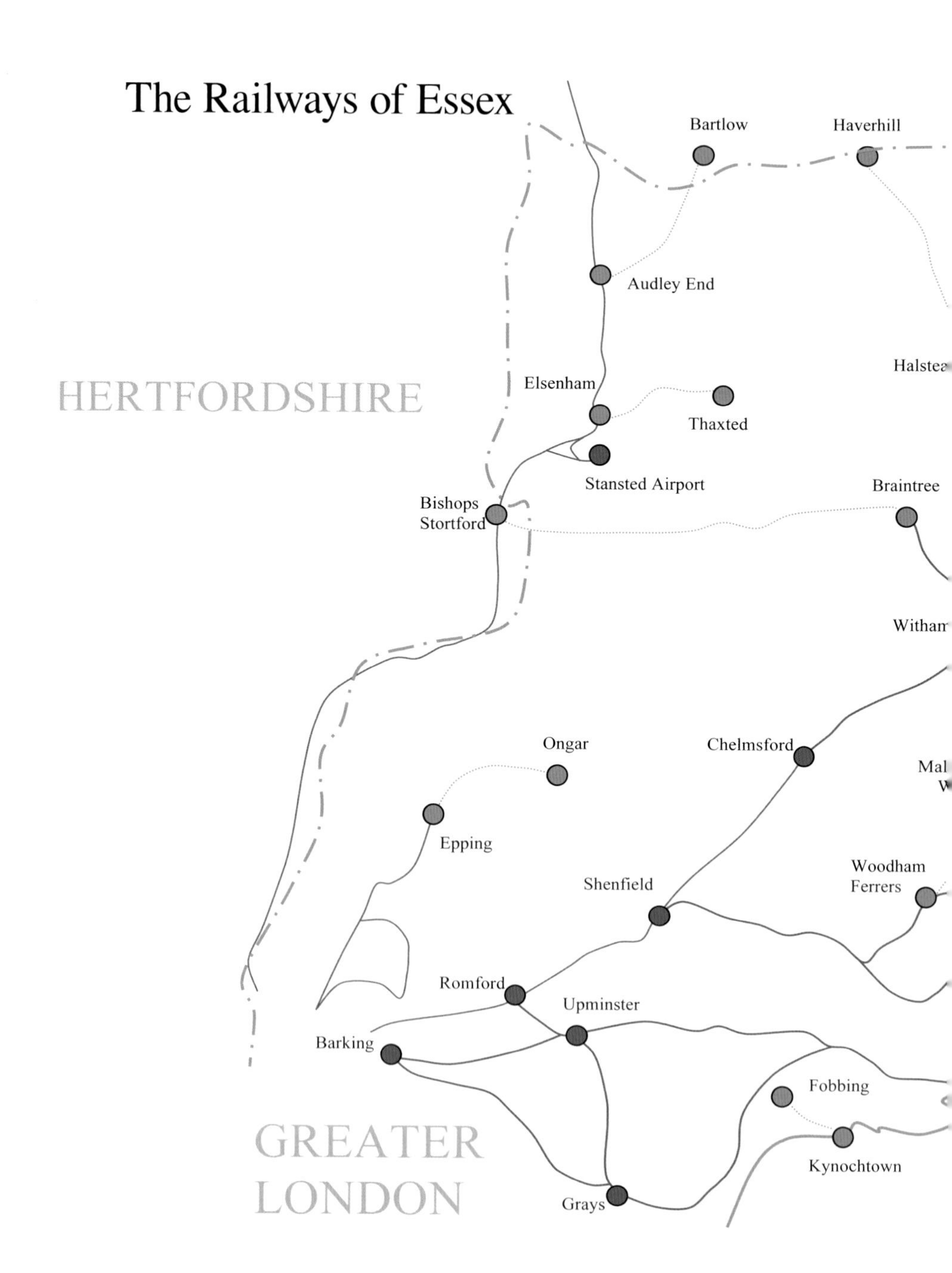
The Railways of Essex
Bartlow
Haverhill
Audley End
HERTFORDSHIRE
Elsenham
Thaxted
Stansted Airport
Braintree
Bishops
Stortford
Ongar
Chelmsford
Epping
Woodham
Ferrers
Shenfield
Romford
Upminster
Barking
Fobbing
Kynochtown
GREATER
LONDON
Grays

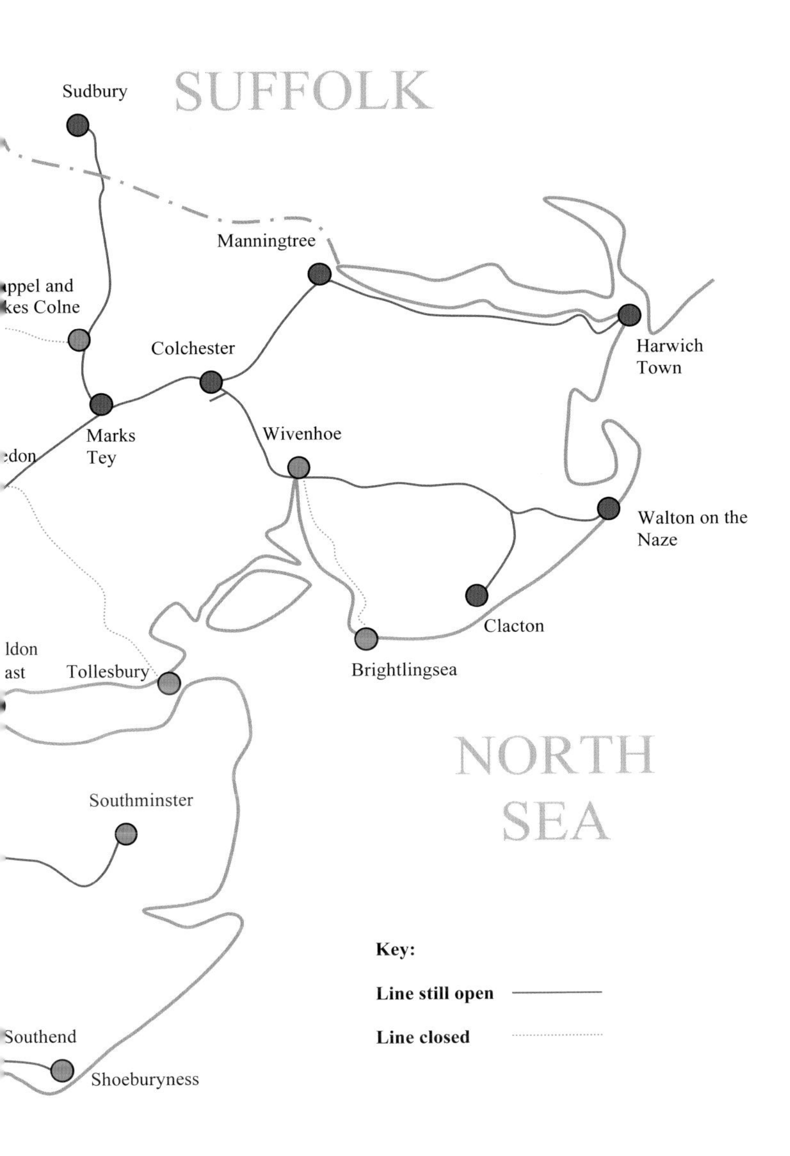
SUFFOLK
Sudbury
Manningtree
Colchester
Marks
Tey
Wivenhoe
Harwich
Town
Walton on the
Naze
Clacton
Brightlingsea
Tollesbury
NORTH
SEA
Southminster
Southend
Shoeburyness
Key:
Line still open
Line closed

A Brief History of the Railways

The railways in the UK have evolved over the years not as part of any grand plan but more as a reaction to technological advances and economic need. The development of the steam engine during the Industrial Revolution created both the need and the way to transport heavy loads over large distances for the first time. Later the dramatic impact of two World Wars helped to bring about even more far-reaching changes in the rail network, as did the growing economic realities of the 1950s and 60s. However, for the purposes of this book the various phases of development have been split into five key areas.

1840 – 1923 (Pre-Grouping)

In 1825 The Stockton and Darlington Railway opened and was the first line to run entirely under the power of steam. From then onwards anyone with enough money could effectively build and run a railway – and they did. During this great period of Victorian industrialisation up to 130 independent railway companies sprang up with such names as The Eastern Counties Railway (ECR), The Colne Valley and Halstead Railway and The Saffron Walden Railway. Some companies ran a single line while others ran several.

In Essex the first railway was opened in 1839 by the ECR and ran from Liverpool Street to Romford. At this time there was very little standardisation across this growing network and until various Railways Acts passed through Parliament, very little in the way of safety inspections or basic working standards. The first big change to this free for all situation came during the First World War when as an economy measure the government effectively took over control of all the railways. With this control came the realisation that the previous unregulated situation had to change.

The Light Railway Act of 1896

The Act was drawn up to help the depressed rural areas of the UK by allowing the construction of quicker and cheaper railways without the need for specific legislation for each line, thereby speeding up the whole process. These new 'Light Railways' were built to a lower overall standard than traditional railways. These standards included: lighter weight track, steeper gradients, tighter curves and a maximum weight of 12 tonnes per axel. Other limitations included a maximum speed of 25 mph (nearer to 10mph approaching level crossings and bends) no trackside signalling and often mixed use of rolling stock where both passenger and goods wagons would be coupled together. On board the train there was only one class of travel and tickets would be issued by the guard or conductor.

Essex had three Light Railways and of those two appear in this book: Elsenham to Thaxted and Kelevdon to Tollesbury. Both of these lines were single track with smaller stations (or halts) along the routes. With only one engine working these lines the trains would often run as a push/pull service with little or no signalling equipment.

1923 – 1945 (Grouping)

It was decided that all current railway companies should be merged into just four large geographic groups. This 'grouping' created the great railway names of our past. The companies were: Southern Railway (SR), London and North East Railway (LNER), Great Western Railway (GWR), and The London, Midland and Scottish Railway (LMS). All came into effect in January 1923. If the railways ever had a golden age then this was it. During this period competition between the LNER and LMS created the high speed routes between London and Scotland culminating in a new steam speed record of 126mph, achieved by the famous Mallard locomotive. A record that still stands to this day.

In Essex the LNER reigned supreme, at a stroke taking over all the independent railways including both the Saffron Walden and Colne Valley and Halstead branch lines. With the outbreak of the Second World War the four railway groups effectively worked together again as both an economy measure and also in a bid to help with the war effort.

1945 – 1962 (Nationalisation to Modernisation)

After World War Two the railways were in a sorry state, suffering from not only the damage wrought by the conflict but also years of underinvestment. The new Labour Government of Clement Atlee proposed to bring the post-war railways under direct state control and to do so created the British Transport Commission (part of which was British Railways) in 1947. In January 1948 the new nationalised railways were born, with ambitious plans to build over 900 new steam engines. By 1955 a new 'Modernisation Plan' was devised whereby £1.5 billion was to be spent over the next 15 years upgrading the network. The main aim was to replace the steam engine with new electric and diesel rolling stock and also to build huge new marshalling yards to encourage more freight traffic. The late 1950s saw British Railways (BR) incur significant losses. This was due in part to both increased car use by the public and a trend towards moving freight on the road network rather than rail. These losses continued year on year until the early 1960s when the Government of Harold Macmillan decided that the railways had to be made to pay their way.

Losses at British Rail (source The National Archive)

1960	£ - 67,000,000
1961	£ - 87,000,000
1962	£ -104,000,000

1963 The Beeching Report

The Conservative Government commissioned a report by the then Chairman of British Rail, Dr Richard Beeching into the future of the railways. Published in March 1963 the Beeching Report stated that 80% of all the traffic was being carried on only 20% of the network and that the only way forward was to dramatically cut back the branch network and to invest in the mainline structures instead. Beeching also wanted more focus to be put on the new containerised freight system along with a greater emphasis on the Inter-City services.

The report recommended that the rail network should be reduced from 13,000 to 11,000 miles and 2,350 stations closed down. The Government accepted the Beeching Report and immediately began to implement its findings. In fact, even after a change of government in 1965 the Labour administration continued with the line closures suggested by Dr Beeching. Most of the branch lines in this book were shutdown during this period from the mid to late 1960s. The most notable exceptions to this were the two Light Railways from Elsenham to Thaxted and Kelvedon to Tollesbury which actually perished in the 1950s. Meanwhile not every branch under threat ended up being closed; the lines from Marks Tey to Sudbury and Witham to Braintree have survived and prosper to this day.

Railway Posters

Today we see the railway poster in very simplistic terms that usually focus on either the quickest way to get from A to B or as a way of keeping us up to date with the latest ticket prices or special offers. But in the 1920s and 30s things were very different. Railways offered a sense of adventure with trips to far-flung places, seaside excursions, or the chance to explore the countryside. During this period the railway poster became an art form. Famous artists were commissioned to show off the destinations offered by the competing big four railway companies with quite often beautiful and striking images. Literally thousands of such posters were created over the years and the following pages contain just a few of the best images that were used to showcase both Essex and East Anglia. All images are courtesy of the National Railway Museum.

L N E R
GREGORY BROWN
EPPING FOREST
QUICKLY REACHED FROM
LIVERPOOL STREET

Nº4 SEA BATHING
EAST COAST JOYS
travel by L·N·E·R
TO THE DRIER SIDE OF BRITAIN

ESSEX
"RAMBLES IN ESSEX"
Illustrated book (with maps)
from stations and bookstalls
1/-
BRITISH RAILWAYS

BUTLIN'S H
CLACTO
IT'S QU

BUTLIN'S
CLACTON
HOLIDAY CAMP
TRUE INTENT IS ALL FOR YOUR DELIGHT
IDAY CAMP
-ON-SEA
BY RAIL

SENTINELS of
BRITAIN'S BEAUTY
ORFORDNESS
REMEMBER
EAST ANGLIA
NEXT SUMMER
Booklet from L·N·E·R Offices & Agents
READ NOW
VISIT LATER

Understanding the Walks

These walks are of varying distance from about 3 to 8 miles and follow a combination of footpaths, established tracks, byways or public roads on circular routes. Essex is by no means a flat county and some of the walks will have their more challenging sections. However, there is nothing too mountainous here and a decent pair of walking shoes should be enough for most people. Many footpaths are clearly marked, though there may be occasions where the signage is lost or missing and you may consider taking the appropriate Ordinance Survey map, listed on each walk, with you as reference. I have also tried to keep these walks off-road as far as possible. However, there are times when you will have to use quiet country lanes and very occasionally cross a busy road. Please beware of traffic at these places.

Although these are essentially railway walks I have tried to include as much local interest as possible, so most walks will take in local villages, churches, pubs and places of interest. The notes for this local information should be read in parallel with the walking directions. Depending on the age and quality of the former rail bed and the existence of buildings, some walks are easier to spot that others; for example, the former Bishops Stortford to Braintree line has now become a designated trail called the Flitch Way and much of the old railway infrastructure is still clearly visible. However, the former light railways in this book were by their very nature less durable constructions and have very little remaining. On these walks careful study of the notes in this book will help you to see points of interest.

Of course some lines still have trains running (Marks Tey to Sudbury) so there will be no problem here. And please remember that some former station houses are now private property and should be treated as such.

Finally, as you may have gathered these are not just railway walks but are also about the villages and communities that surround them. So don't expect each walk to stick to the actual railway line (the footpaths do not always allow for that) but rather that each one will wander on and off the course of the railway at various points with detours into villages and places of interest. By exploring the surrounding communities and countryside I hope you will be able to appreciate why the railways came to these far flung places, how challenging their construction must have been, and maybe even why they eventually disappeared.

Supporting rural pubs

Please try to visit the dozens of great country pubs that are present in the pages of this book. Many of them have wonderful character as well as good food and drink and are an integral part of their local communities. Rural pubs are closing at an alarming rate (one or two have disappeared during the writing of this book) and the best thing that you can do to support them is to drop in when you can during your walks and enjoy their hospitality.

Get your timing right....

Some of the walks here will give you the chance to visit such local attractions as railway museums or gardens along the way. I have tried to include as many points of interest as possible. If you intend to visit some of these attractions then do check the opening times of each attraction before you set off (details should be on the opening page of each walk) and you will then be able to make maximum use of your time.

Abbreviations

I have borrowed some common abbreviations from the cross-country running community to help shorten any long paragraphs of directions. They are repeated throughout this book and are as follows:

L	= left
R	= right
TL	= turn left
TR	= turn right
SA	= straight ahead
FPS*	= footpath sign
LHFE	= left hand field edge
RHFE	= right hand field edge
LHFC	= left hand field corner
RHFC	= right hand field corner

* For the purposes of this book a footpath sign is any official signage pointing along a public right of way. When you read FPS in the directions it will denote official signage including: waymark posts, byway, bridleway directions and footpath signs.

The Walks

Epping to Ongar

The Eastern Counties Railway extended its line from Liverpool Street out to the leafy pastures of Ongar in 1865 when the six mile long Epping to Ongar branch opened. With intermediate stations at North Weald and Blake Hall the single track ran under steam power through several changes of ownership until eventually becoming part of the London Underground system where it was ultimately electrified in 1957.

Despite plans to extend the line to Dunmow, Ongar remained the end of the line. For various reasons the branch never really saw high passenger numbers and was often under the threat of closure. Blake Hall (the least used station on the whole network) was closed in 1981 and the introduction of new computerised trains in the early 1990s meant that the line needed either substantial upgrading or closure. London Underground unsurprisingly went for the latter and the line closed in 1994, taking with it North Weald and Ongar stations.

All the station buildings are still standing and can be found on the walks in this chapter, while Epping is still a working station and is now the terminus of the Central Line. At the other end of the line a small band of dedicated enthusiasts called the Epping Ongar Railway Volunteer Society has dedicated itself to running a heritage railway along the old branch and now operates services from Ongar on to North Weald and Coopersale on most Sundays (except during the winter). If you want to combine the walks in this chapter with a visit to the heritage railway please check the EOR* website for more information.

*The Epping to Ongar Railway:

Tel: 01277 365200
Web: www.eorailway.co.uk

Epping

Distance: 5 miles
Map: OS Explorer 174 (GR 459021)

Getting there:

Epping station is at the eastern end of the Central Line with regular arrivals and departures towards London. By car, it is on the B1393 and can be accessed from the M11 by using either junction 5 or 7.

Parking:

Use either the station car park or the pay and display off St Johns Road, close to the High Road.

Pubs on route:

The Garnon Bushes in Coopersale
The Theydon Oak in Coopersale Street

Route map

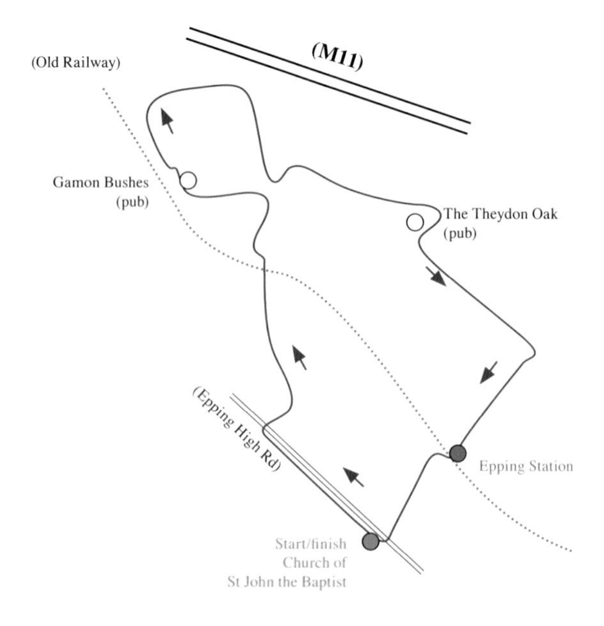

The Walk

Starting with a stroll along the High Road then it's off, cross country to Coopersale where we meet the railway several times before joining the Essex Way, returning to Epping via the railway station.

Start at the junction of St Johns Road and the High Road with the Church of St John the Baptist behind you. TL to walk along High Road and pass the Council offices on your L. Continue SA out of town past a small green on your L, cross the main road and TR up Stonards Hill Rd. Opposite Theydon Grove Rd TL and follow FPS across recreation ground, pass first a tennis court and then a football pitch on L and head for the RHFC. Go SA on an enclosed track for 200yds following a good track keeping buildings on your L, go through gate and follow footpath SA. (The line of trees ahead mark the old railway track). Cross railway at bridge and TL following FP for 200yds. Exit onto road and immediately TR for 100yds and at FPS TR for another 50yds.

Now TL onto main road and walk through Coopersale passing the pub (Garnon Bushes) with the old railway bridge ahead. Just before bridge TR along Garnon Mead and after 200yds TL at a kissing gate which is marked Nature Reserve (don't go to the main entrance 100yds further along the road) go through gate and proceed SA through woods to eventually crossing a plank bridge. The railway should be to your L. Keep to this footpath which eventually bears round to the R (as the railway goes L) until you reach a tarmac road. TL and go SA towards the roar of the M11 and follow the track with the motorway on your L.

At FPS TR for 200yds and at next FPS TL across wooden bridge. Go SA following the Essex Way through woods, passing a school on your R. At FPS by a gate TL to continue through the woods heading downhill via some wide steps. At FPS TR to exit woods into a field and go SA keeping to field edge, cross into next field and as before keep to RHFE.

After 300yds at next FPS TL across field, go through hedge into next field and keep to RHFE. TR at FPS and cross the field towards the road. TR onto road and pass the pub (The Theydon Oak) and keep to the LH main road.

At the post box and telephone TL at FPS and follow the track slightly uphill (this can get very muddy in wet weather) and continue for about ½ mile to reach a main road. TR onto road for 20yds and at FPS TR into field and follow RHFE, pass through a gap in the hedge and follow the track uphill towards Epping. Keep L following the enclosed track with houses on your L, and at road TR for 50yds then TL down a dead-end road to reach footbridge over railway.

Cross bridge to reach Epping station. With the station behind you TR and proceed up the approach road (you can stop here to see the old track from the roadbridge) and then TL up Station Road towards the town centre. When you reach the High Road TR and you are back at the church on St Johns Road.

Epping Station early 1900s (NRM collection)

Epping 2009 (author)

Steam and electric together at Epping back in the 1950s (Lens of Sutton)

North Weald

Distance: 5 miles
Map: OS Explorer 174 and 183 (GR 497036)

Getting there:

North Weald is on the B181 between Epping and Ongar

Parking:

Parking should be available along Station Road, also you may be able to use the pub car park or nearby side streets.

Pubs:

The Kings Head on the High Road close to Station Road
The Green Man in Toot Hill

Route Map

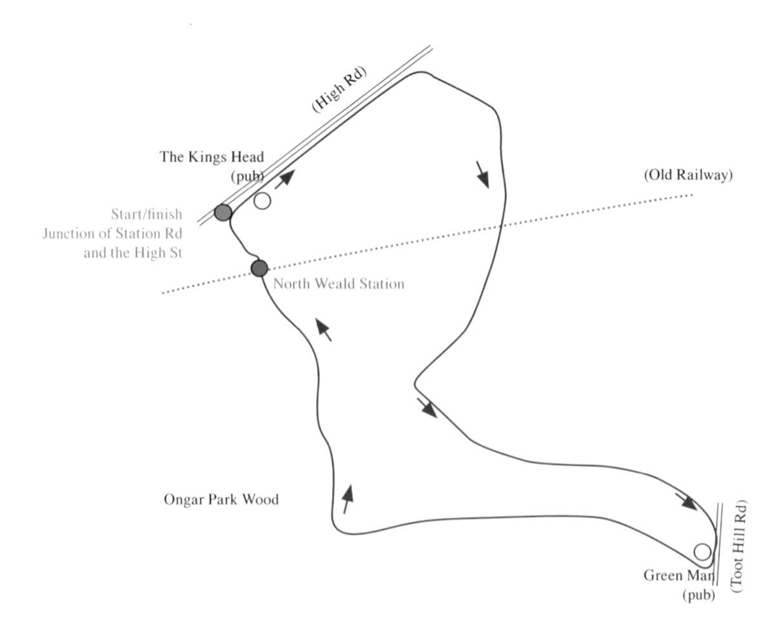

The Walk

Starting with a walk away from the station and up the High Road before moving on to Toot Hill and the Green Man pub. From here we join the Essex Way towards Ongar Park Woods before arriving at the railway and North Weald station.

With your back to Station Road TR along the High Rd passing the pub (Kings Head) Post Office and local shops. After about ½ mile pass School Green Lane on L. At next bend in the main road TR at FPS and follow the tarmac track for 500yds. At FPS TR across field to stile and cross next field diagonally with concrete blocks on your L until you reach a hedge on your R. Keep to RHFE until you reach a road. TR onto road and immediately follow it as it bears L towards communication tower.

Cross the railway using bridge and go SA to the end of the road and use gate to enter field (beside cottage). Follow track across field to gate (stay in same field) and follow LHFE to a set of steps. TL going SA towards wood, and follow FPS to proceed SA through wood passing a fishing lake on your L. On leaving wood, follow a good track between fields and head towards farm buildings. At water tower go SA onto road (Mill Lane) and pass Clunes House on your R, continue SA to next junction and TR to follow road through Toot Hill.

Pass the Green Man pub and after 50yds TR at FPS and follow track across field to stile. Follow RHFE ahead for 300yds to field corner. At FPS bear L and cross next field diagonally to reach another FPS hidden in hedge. TL and follow good track across field for about ½ mile to reach Ongar Park Wood. At FPS TR towards North Weald and keep the woods to your L. At field corner and FPS follow the track diagonally across next field (away from woods) and you should now be able to see North Weald Station to your L in the distance.

Cross road and at FPS turn slightly L and walk downhill with the hedge on your L. As you approach the station cross stile and railway track (be careful – trains sometimes run here) follow the footpath round to the approach road. TL onto Station Lane and walk back to the junction with the High Road.

North Weald in the 1930s (Lens of Sutton)

The last train service in 1994 (author)

The Green Man pub Toot Hill

Ongar and Blake Hall

Distance: 6½ miles approx
Map: OS Explorer 183 and 174 (GR 552031)

Getting there:

Ongar is just off the A414 between Epping and Chelmsford. The A414 can also be accessed from junction 7 of the M11.

Parking:

There is a long stay car park next to the library

Pubs on route:

The Cock Tavern, Ongar High Street
The Royal Oak, Ongar High Street

Route Map

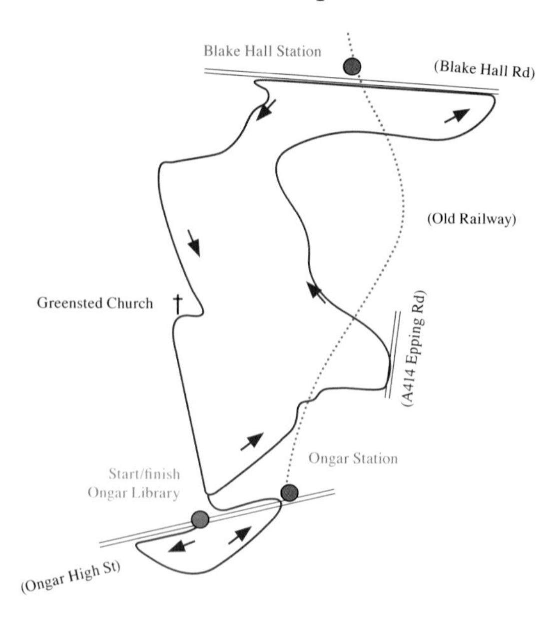

The Walk

This is a longer walk that starts with a quick tour of Ongar, visiting the old railway station before heading off towards Blake Hall crossing the old track no fewer than four times. The route visits the charming hamlet of Greensted Green and then joins the Essex Way to return to Ongar via historic Greensted Church.

With the library behind you TL up the High Street. Just before the Post Office TL up Castle Street for 300yds to FPS at the end of the road. (Just past the Post Office is the Royal Oak pub). Follow footpath SA on a good track passing a pond on your L. At next FPS TL through kissing gate and go SA past old castle moat on L. Follow this main path (don't TL through castle) and pass the scout hut on R. At end of track TL onto tarmac road and continue down to the main road ahead. Cross this road to see Ongar Station on the R. (Station may be fenced off when not open). Check the Ongar Railway Preservation Society website (www.eorailway.co.uk) or telephone, (01277 365200) for more information.

With the station behind you TR back towards Ongar along the High Street until you reach the library. TR into Bansons Lane, pass the supermarket on L and follow the track downhill, crossing the river. Go SA and slightly uphill for 100yds and at corner of hedge TR following a line of trees. Follow this track as it meets up with the old railway line (Ongar Station is on your R) and turns L along field edge. At field corner cross concrete bridge into next field and then TR to pass under the railway using a bridge.

Go SA for 30yds and TL to follow track with river on your R. Continue this route as the river approaches the main road ahead. At road TL and go SA for 100yds keeping to hedge, and at FPS TL along good track going uphill.

Follow this track until you cross the railway using bridge and continue SA. At cottage go SA into woods and continue along this enclosed track (Pensons Lane). On reaching a road look for a FPS on R and follow enclosed track with a house on R for about 50yds to reach a field. Go across field bearing slightly L towards a thicket of trees ahead and then cross to another thicket on the R (footpath may be indistinct here) and head for a line of trees that mark the railway track.

At gap in bushes drop down to stile and cross the railway (watch out – trains still run here) and emerge into the next field. Head across the field bearing to your R to keep close to the wooded area (footpath is hard to see here but eventually a track can be found as you head downhill). You are aiming for the cottage ahead at the bottom of the hill. When track reaches a concrete road follow it round to the L to reach the main road. TL on the road and follow it uphill. At the crest of the hill you will reach the former Blake Hall station, which is now a private residence.

Cross the bridge and proceed SA on road until you reach the next junction. TL up Pensons Lane and after 50yds take the R fork down a good track and at FPS on R follow enclosed track SA. At FPS TR and go SA with a row of trees on your R until you cross a wooden bridge to reach a FPS by a road. TL onto road for 50yds to reach another FPS on L. Follow this path (Essex Way) keeping to the LHFE, pass wood on L and cross wooden bridge into next field. Continue SA until a wooden bridge brings you to a good track. TR onto track for 50yds then go through gate, passing wooden houses on your L to reach Greensted Church up ahead. (This very old church is well worth a visit).

Just past the church TL at FPS and follow road for 50yds to a gate and go SA on grass track until you reach a FPS in a small thicket of trees. Follow track SA across middle of field (Ongar is straight ahead) and finally cross over the river, pass the supermarket on your R and walk back towards the library up ahead and the end of the walk.

Ongar Station 2009 (author)

The approach to Ongar around 1911 (NRM collection)

Blake Hall 1911 (NRM collection)

Blake Hall 2009 (author)

Greensted Church

Woodham Ferrers to Maldon West

Constructed by the Great Eastern Railway the single track, nine mile branch line opened in 1889 to provide this remote part of Essex with a link to the London and Southend Victoria mainline service which also opened in the same year. From Maldon West trains would either travel to Maldon East or direct to Witham.

Originally there was only one intermediate station (at Cold Norton). An attempt was made in the 1920s to boost passenger numbers by adding two new halts at Stow St Mary and Barons Lane (near Purleigh). However, the line was still poorly used and the half dozen or so trains that ran daily were temporarily suspended as an economy measure during the Second World War – never to reopen to passengers. Freight services continued after the war but the branch line finally closed to all traffic in the 1950s.

Today much has been lost of this old branch line. The stations at Cold Norton, Barons Lane and Maldon West have long since been demolished, but the tiny halt at Stow Maries still has its clinker platform and railway bridge and is now part of the local nature reserve. Much of the trackbed and several of the roadbridges are still present and form part of the forthcoming walk in this book. Woodham Ferrers is still a working station.

Stow Maries and Cold Norton

Distance: 5½ miles approx

Map: OS Explorer 183 and 175 (GR 842021)

Getting there:

Purleigh is on the B1010 and is close to Maldon, Danbury and South Woodham Ferrers

Parking:

You may be able to park at the Bell Pub (please ask first). Otherwise you can park with consideration on any of the surrounding streets

Pub on route:

The Bell on The Street, Purleigh

Route Map

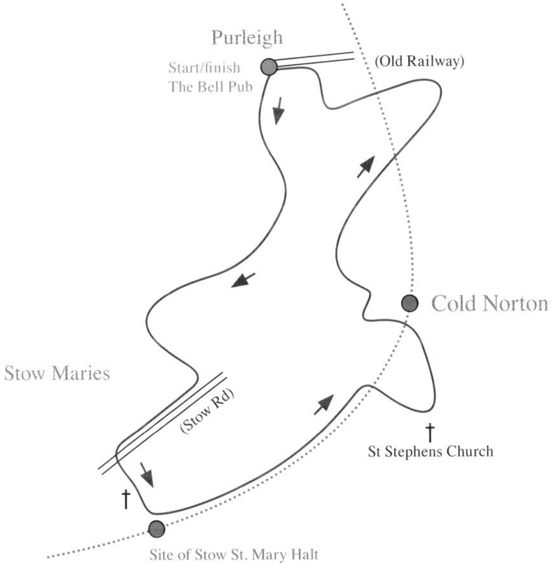

Purleigh
Start/finish
The Bell Pub
(Old Railway)
Cold Norton
Stow Maries
(Stow Rd)
St Stephens Church
Site of Stow St. Mary Halt

The Walk

Starting at the highest point in the village of Purleigh then it's off to Stow Maries and a long walk along the old railway formation before visiting Cold Norton and returning to Purleigh and the Bell pub.

Stand with the Bell pub behind you and TR up The Street (don't follow the road downhill) ignore the FPS beside pub and go SA to a concrete road and pass Purleigh Hall. Go SA to stile and continue across next field to FPS in hedge. At this junction of footpaths go SA following track across the middle of field. Cross wooden bridge onto enclosed track and go SA crossing next field keeping to LHFE. At the top of field TL onto road and go SA for 200yds to find a FPS on the R by gate. Follow track uphill keeping to RHFE until you are about 2/3rds of the way across field where you should TL following a good track across field towards the water tower. (Turn around here – there are good views towards Maldon).

Follow track behind the water tower to reach a road. TR onto road for 200yds and at next junction follow the road on left (Hagg Hill) and follow this quiet lane downhill to reach Stow Road.TR onto Stow Road keeping to footpath and walk through the village of Stow Maries. Pass Honeypot Lane until you reach Church Lane on L. Turn down this lane, passing the church until you finally cross the old railway track using a brick bridge. Just over the bridge TR down the embankment to bring you onto the old track-bed. (Stow Maries Nature Reserve can be visited here). You will also find the remains of the old Stow St Mary Halt beside the track-bed (all that is left is a few wooden sleepers and the raised earth base).

Now walk under the bridge and continue along the course of the old railway, heading towards Cold Norton.

As you walk you will pass a large golf course on both sides of the railway. Go SA for up to a mile (bypassing a demolished overbridge) and eventually the footpath will end where you will reach a disused bridge at a road. Go up onto the road and TR heading uphill until you reach a church (St Stephens). TL at FPS and go to gate behind church. Take the footpath that goes SA (not to R) and follow the track towards the trees ahead. Continue SA on enclosed track until you reach the main road. TL and cross old railway bridge.

To the right of this bridge is where Cold Norton station was sited. This substantial building has long been demolished but the Stationmasters House may still remain. Follow the main road through the village (pass the old pub on L) for 300yds to reach FPS on R (Crown Road). Follow this track SA for 300yds to FPS and TL crossing field to another FPS, TR and follow enclosed track to gate. Go SA keeping to LHFE to reach a kissing gate. Now keep to RHFE for 200yds before bearing slightly L to reach a stile. TR and follow a good gravel track for about 1/3 mile. The old railway track will cross your path at right angles but you should continue SA on the gravel track towards the farm ahead and Roundbush Road.

On reaching the road TL (past Lower Barn Farm) for 20yds to reach FPS where you should TL and follow the track across field. At field corner turn slightly L and cross next field heading towards a row of trees that mark the route of the old railway. At FPS go up steps to cross railway and continue SA across next field. Just before telegraph pole in field TR and follow track towards the road. TL onto road and proceed SA back into Purleigh and the Bell pub.

A rare picture of the Stow St Mary halt possibly around 1930

The Bell pub, Purleigh (author)

Witham to Maldon East

Sited on the Thames Estuary close to both the Chelmer and Blackwater rivers Maldon had not one, but two railway stations: Maldon East and Maldon West. Running into Maldon East was the Maldon, Witham and Braintree Railway. Originally planned as a double track (reduced to single in the 1850s) the line gave the ancient port and its surrounding fruit growing areas direct access to Witham and onwards via the main line to both London and Cambridge. Intermediate stations were at Wickham Bishops and Langford. The Maldon East station building was a grand, imposing structure built in Jacobean style with a nine arch entrance arcade.

Goods services were of great importance to the railway, particularly fresh produce from local farms as well as incoming canned food offloaded at Maldon, and this to some extent kept the line running. As with other branch lines the Beeching Report saw it as loss making and proposed its closure. Passenger services finished in 1964 with goods following in 1966.

Much of the old railway formation still exists between Maldon and Witham, and of particular note are the old Maldon East station building, and the wooden viaducts at Wickham Bishops – both of which feature in up-coming walks. The section of line from Witham to Braintree survived closure and has prospered to this day under electrification.

Don't forget to visit the Museum of Power at Langford. Check their website for opening times:

www.museumofpower.org.uk
Tel: 01621 843183

Maldon East to the Museum of Power in Langford

Distance: 4¾ miles approx
Map: OS Explorer 183 (GR 854075)

Getting there:

By car Maldon is best accessed from the Hatfield Peveral junction of the A12. Maldon East station is on Station Road, just off the A414 in Maldon. Nearest railway stations are Hatfield Peveral or Witham

Parking:

Parking should be possible along Station Road

Food and drink on route:

The Welcome pub, Fullbridge, Maldon. Museum of Power, Langford

Route Map

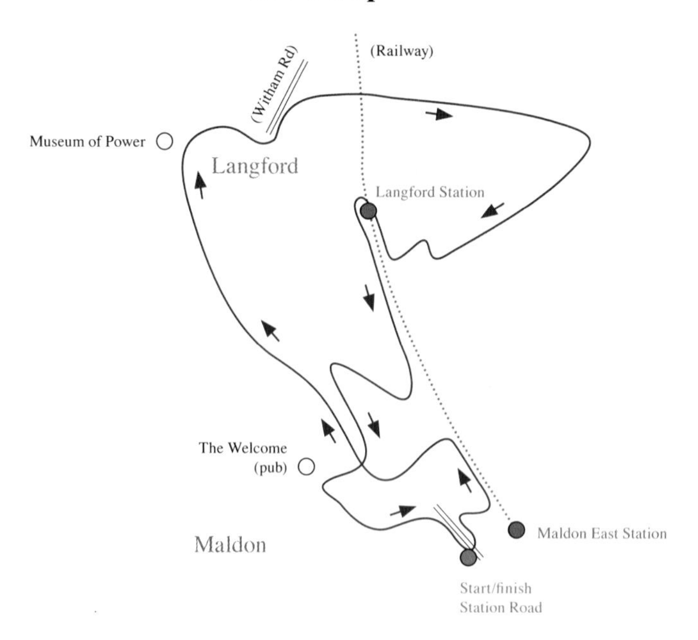

The Walk

The walk starts at the grade one listed Maldon East station before following the Langford Cut to the Museum of Power and then visiting the site of the old Langford station. We then follow the route of the railway back into Maldon via the Welcome pub.

Start on Station Road outside the old station building. The station now has listed status and is used for office accommodation. With the station behind you TR up the road towards the roundabout. At the roundabout TR and immediately cross the road to reach the old Maldon Ironworks building. TR and head for the next roundabout and when you reach it TL following signs for the A12 to Colchester. (This dual carriageway follows the old railway route from Witham to Maldon). Keep to the left and cross bridge over the Langford Cut and after 50yds TL onto a concrete road going down into a park.

Pass the gate and immediately TL following the track towards the river, passing a pond on your R. On reaching the tarmac path TR and follow it SA. Stay on this path to cross the Cut using a footbridge and then TR at the footpath junction, leading you through reed beds and bringing you to the water's edge of the Cut. TL and follow this waterside track as it passes beneath the main road. (This road follows the exact route from the old Maldon West to East Stations railway line). Stay on the left hand bank of the Cut to pass an old brick bridge and continue SA.

After a while the track becomes a road as you pass Maldon Golf Club on your L. At the floodgates cross Cut using the bridge and follow the road SA. On reaching the main road TL to visit the Museum of Power. (This former Victorian pumping station has a fantastic display of working engines plus a miniature railway. Check the website: www.museumofpower.org.uk for opening times and special events).

On leaving the museum TR along the main road (passing Village Hall on L) and at the church TL onto the Witham Road, keeping to the verge where possible. After 500yds you will reach Langford Hall on your L. TR and follow the FPS that points up a concrete road. (Just ahead of you the old railway followed the row of trees that meets this road and then proceeded to carry on to the L to go under the Witham Road).

Go SA and pass farm buildings and a reservoir on the R. As the track meets the end of the reservoir TR to follow a good path beside a line of trees. As trees end continue SA following LHFE towards road and houses up ahead. On reaching the main road TR (keeping to verge) and head towards the bridge. After 200yds (and before bridge) cross road at FPS and cross field bearing slightly L towards the line of trees that mark the old railway route. At FPS in hedge TR along the old track-bed and proceed SA towards the remains of Langford Station. (The old station house still remains, as does the brick built platform. Although heavily overgrown the old iron railings still exist. The station opened in 1848.)
Now turn around and retrace your steps back along the track-bed and continue SA until the main road runs parallel to you on your L. About 500yds further along you will reach a divide in the footpaths and you should take the R track (slightly downhill) to a FPS. Cross the field ahead towards a brick bridge in the distance. Do not cross bridge but TL to follow the track beside the water until you pass under the road bridge to reach One Tree Meadow.

Go SA keeping to the water's edge, pass under footbridge and immediately TL and follow the path as it brings to up and over the footbridge (supermarket on your L). Follow the path on your L to reach the highest point, overlooking the River Chelmer and continue L along the rivers edge. At the end of the path you will reach a road (Bridge Court). TR to follow the river and pass the pub (The Welcome) on your L. At the main road (Fullbridge), TL and go SA for 200yds to reach a roundabout. Finally TR up Station Road for 200yds to bring you back to Maldon East Station and the end of your walk.

Maldon East station 2009 (author)

Museum of Power, Langford (author)

Langford station around 1910 (William H Smith)

Langford station 2009 (author)

Wickham Bishops

Distance: 5 miles
Map: OS Explorer 183 (GR 847122)

Getting there:

Use the Hatfield Peveral exit of the A12, follow the B1019 towards Maldon then look for local signs to Wickham Bishops. The nearest stations are either Hatfield Peveral or Witham

Parking:

There is a small car park outside the Mitre pub

Pubs on route:

The Mitre and The Chequers pubs are both on The Street, Wickham Bishops

Route Map

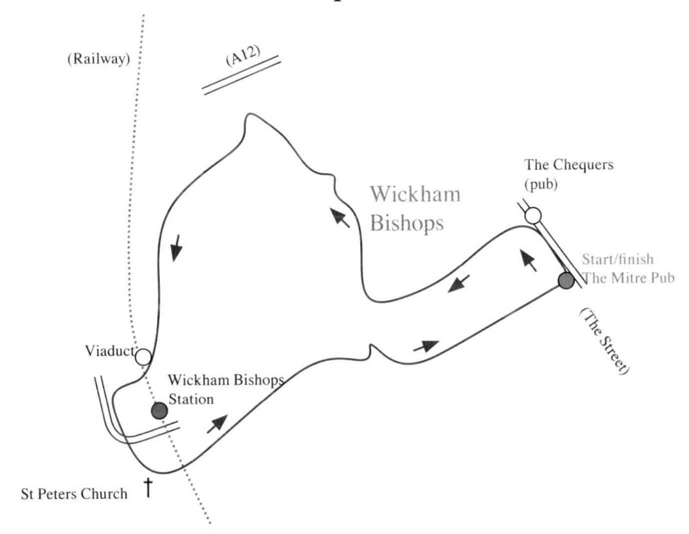

The Walk

This walk takes a journey from the higher ground of Wickham Bishops, down past the Golf Club to reach the UK's oldest surviving wooden railway viaduct as it crosses the River Blackwater. We then bypass the old station and return to the village via St Peters Church and surrounding fruit orchards.

Start at the Mitre pub on The Street in Wickham Bishops. With the pub behind you TR up The Street passing the local shops and Post Office. When you reach The Chequers pub TL down Church Road. At next main road junction TR and proceed SA towards the church. Pass the church and after 100yds TR up Mope Lane. (There are two footpath signs on this road – ignore the first one you come to). After 400yds TL at FPS and follow the enclosed track to reach a kissing gate at a small wood. TR and follow the track as it works its way around the edge of the wood and cross a wooden bridge to reach another kissing gate. Follow the track downhill across field to reach a hedge.

Go SA to emerge onto a golf course and follow the gravel track downhill as it bears to the L. (There should be small FPSs along the way). At the bottom corner of the golf course follow the track round to the L and continue SA on gravel track. Eventually the track turns to grass but carry on through the golf course with the river (Blackwater) or your R. Cross over a weir and follow FPS SA to exit the golf course at a gate. Follow the track close to the river to reach the old wooden viaduct. (Essex County Council renovated this viaduct, and another on private land to the left, in 1995 and they are now listed as 'Ancient Monuments'. There were several other viaducts on this branch line but they have long since been demolished).

Now carry on SA and follow the footpath round to reach a dirt road beside a house. Follow this road round to the R until it reaches the main road ahead. (You will also see the second viaduct across the field on your L. This is on private land.

Look for the display board beside the footpath that charts the history of the railway). Once on the main road TL, cross a bridge and look for a FPS on the R, (behind a post box). Follow the good track SA as it proceeds slightly uphill. (As you walk here look back to your L to see the roadbridge that goes over the old railway track-bed. On the other side of the bridge was the site of Wickham Bishops Station. This is now a private house).

Continue along this track to reach St Peters Church hidden in the trees. Follow the track to the L of the church to bring you to an old railway bridge, cross over and go SA towards the main road. At road go SA to a FPS on opposite side, pass through the gate on L and follow the grass track ahead. Continue uphill, cross a small road and go SA into the next field. Now go SA through the orchard to eventually reach a FPS in the hedge. Emerge onto the road, TL and go SA for 100yds. TR at FPS to go through a kissing gate and follow the track ahead.
On reaching a road (Grange Road) TL and go SA back towards Wickham Bishops. Keep to this larger road to pass the library on your R and keep going SA to reach The Mitre pub on The Street and the end of your walk.

St Peters Church (author)

The restored wooden viaduct at Wickham Bishops (author)

The Chequers pub (author)

Kelvedon to Tollesbury Light Railway

It is easy to see why Arthur Wilkin (of the famous Wilkin and Sons jam factory) was a keen supporter of the railway. Until the line opened in 1904 all the factory produce had to be taken to town by horse and cart along unmade roads making for long and treacherous journeys. This is a perfect example of exactly what the Light Railways were designed to do; unlock the rural areas and allow local producers and farmers to get their wares into town more quickly and efficiently.

The railway ran for almost nine miles with stations at Kelvedon, Feering, Inworth, Tiptree, Tolleshunt Knights, Tolleshunt D'Arcy and Tollesbury. With a further extension being built to Tollesbury Pier in 1907, the railway gained the nickname 'Crab and Winkle' line. Many of the stations were little more that raised clinker platforms with an old railway carriage for a waiting room while the train itself ran on a single track with few signals. In line with other Light Railways steep embankments and expensive earthworks were kept to a minimum while only one bridge was constructed, which still survives to this day. The line seems to have had reasonable goods traffic but generally passenger numbers were light. During the Second World War the Pier extension was destroyed to prevent enemy invasion and was never rebuilt.

With growing car and bus use the railway saw a further decline in passengers and finally the line closed in 1951, while goods traffic continued until 1962. Little remains today of the Kelvedon to Tollesbury railway other than a few raised embankments and one bridge. However, the Wilkin's Jam Factory Museum has a small but very interesting section covering the line; while the remains of Tollesbury Pier can clearly be seen at low tide.

Tollesbury Pier

Distance: 5¾ miles
Map: OS Explorer 176 (GR 956104)

Getting there:
Tollesbury is at the end of the B1023. It is best accessed from the A12 by following signs for Tiptree and then continuing on to Tollesbury. Nearest railway station is Colchester.

Parking:
You should be able to park with care on the streets of the town.

Pubs on route:
The Kings Head, Church Street

Route Map

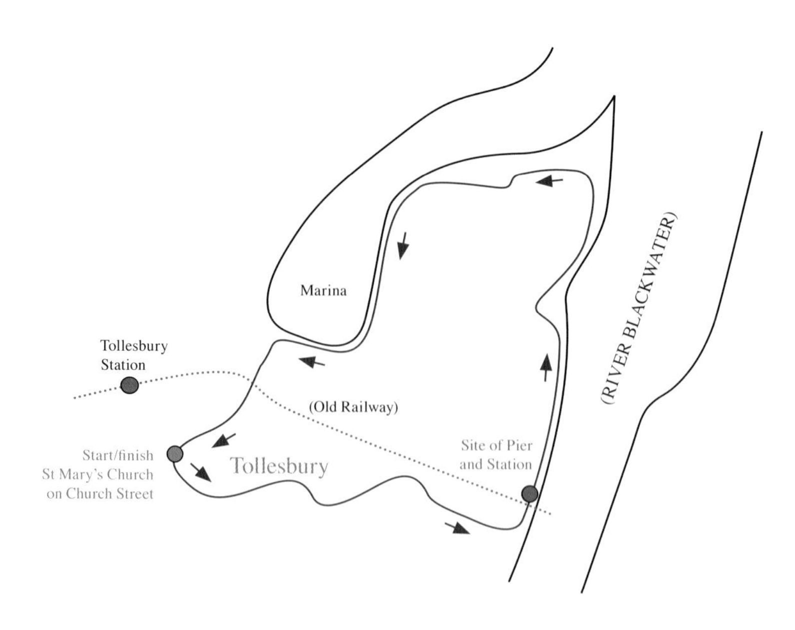

The Walk

This is an interesting walk around Tollesbury following the old Light Railway out to the remains of the former Tollesbury Pier before following the shoreline back to the harbour. (Please undertake this walk at low tide, as this is the only time when you will be able to see the pier foundations.)

Start your walk on Church Road (opposite Station Road junction). Walk past St Mary's Church on your L and follow the road ahead as it bears to the L. After 300yds go SA to pass a FPS on your L and continue on the narrow lane ahead. After another 100yds TL at FPS (by a gate) and go SA into a field. At the field corner TR through a gate and follow the track SA along the RHFE. Cross into another field and continue along the RHFE. On reaching the field corner (with houses on your L) TR onto a narrow lane and proceed SA. After about 200yds the road comes to an end, now TL at FPS and go through a gate to follow the enclosed track ahead. Continue SA as you pass Wick Farm on your L and follow the track as it heads downhill.

Eventually you will reach a FPS on your R. The row of trees ahead of you follows the old railway line. Now TR over the stile to follow the track on the RHFE. At the field corner go up onto the sea wall, pass through a gate on your L and go SA to reach a stile. Cross the stile and proceed SA. (There should be a narrow strip of water on your L, while the hedgerow further over marks the railway formation as it reaches the River Blackwater). Now TL to follow the sea wall as it passes the remains of the old Tollesbury Pier.

You will now follow the sea wall for a long walk back towards the town and marina. Keep to this path with Bradwell Power Station away to your R as the sea wall eventually bears to the L and you can see the marina in the distance. Pass the boatyard on your R and continue SA on a good footpath to cross onto a gravel track to pass Tollesbury Cruising Club on your L.

Now look for a FPS leading to a small gravel track (in front of some white weatherboarded houses) and follow this track to reach a road. TL onto this road and go SA towards the town to finally head uphill to bring you back to Church Street and the end of your walk.

Tollesbury station (on Station Rd) circa 1940. Sadly no longer present. (Lens of Sutton)

The remains of Tollesbury Pier 2009 (author)

Across the creek with Brightlingsea in the distance (author)

Lightship moored at Tollesbury Marina (author)

Tolleshunt Knights

Distance: 3 ½ miles
Map: OS Explorer 184 (GR 907151)

Getting there:
Tolleshunt Knights is on the B1023 between Tiptree and Tolleshunt D'Arcy. Nearest railway station is at Witham.

Parking:
You should be able to park with care on the side roads in the village.

Food and drink on route:
The Rose and Crown pub Tolleshunt Knights. Tea shop and museum at the Wilkin and Sons Jam Factory.

Route Map

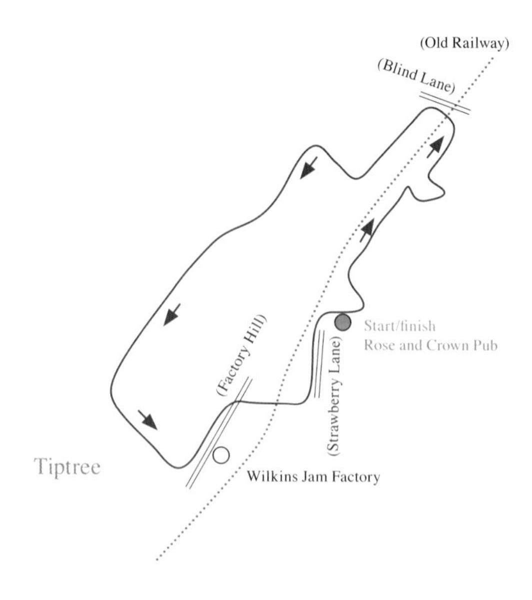

The Walk

This is a short walk over what remains of the old Kelvedon to Tollesbury railway. Starting at Tolleshunt Knights we follow the old railway embankment to reach the only surviving bridge on the line, then it's off cross country to arrive on the outskirts of Tiptree before reaching the Wilkins Jam Factory and its museum.

Start at the Rose and Crown pub on the B1023 which runs through Tolleshunt Knights. (Sadly the old station has long since gone). With the pub behind you TL and follow the main road slightly downhill. After 50yds TL at FPS onto a grassy track and go SA following the LHFE. Cross a stile at the gap in the hedge onto an enclosed track and after 50yds TR at FPS to go through a small wood. (Watch out for horses around here). Cross a plank bridge and go SA across field to yet another stile. (The old railway passes to your L following the hedgerow). Now go SA across the next field to find a FPS hidden in the hedge. Continue SA, crossing several stiles and keeping to the LHFE you will finally reach a stables. Pass to the L of the stables and you will reach a road. TR onto the road and after 200yds TL at FPS to follow the road towards the Village Hall.

Once you reach the car park TL and pass the hall on your R. Keeping to the LHFE go to the top corner of the field and then TR to follow the field edge. At the FPS up ahead pass through the hedge to follow the track between houses to reach a road (Blind Lane). TL and follow the lane as it crosses the old railway bridge. (This is the only bridge left from the old railway and is certainly a testament to the strength of Staffordshire blue bricks from which it is made. Fired to a much higher temperature than standard bricks, these incredibly strong blue bricks can still be found up and down the country on old railway and canal structures).

Continue along Blind Lane to reach a road junction ahead. TL onto Rectory Road and go SA to reach the outskirts of the village.

At the main road junction ahead TL to follow the road SA. As you exit the village TR at FPS and follow the RHFE. At field corner cross a plank bridge into the next field, TL and follow the LHFE. Cross into the next field and go SA until you reach a fishing lake on your R. Now go SA to follow the LHFE (away from the lake) and go SA crossing into another field towards the wood up ahead. Follow the track SA to pass a small copse on your L as you head uphill towards a wood.

Go through Birch Wood and finally pass to the L of some houses. Exit onto the main road and TL (passing a church on the R) to proceed SA towards a junction ahead. At the junction (by Police Station) TL and follow the road (Factory Hill) out of Tiptree. After a short walk you will find the entrance to the Wilkins Jam Factory, Tea Shop and Visitor Centre. (This is well worth a visit as the Museum has a display on the history of the railway).

Now leave the factory and TR to follow Factory Hill out of town. After 300yds you will reach a road junction, TR down Tudwick Road and continue SA. (The railway crossed the road along here as it leaves the jam factory, but all traces seem to have been lost). Reaching some houses you will come to a junction where you should TL onto Strawberry Lane. Continue along this lane as you come back into the village to finally reach the junction with the B1023 D'Arcy Road. TR onto this road to bring you back to the Rose and Crown pub and the end of your walk.

Tiptree station 1950, sadly no longer present (NRM collection)

The only remaining bridge of the branch at Blind Lane (author)

The Rose and Crown pub, Tolleshunt Knights (author)

The Wilkin jam factory was a great supporter of the railway (author)

Bishops Stortford to Braintree

Originally proposed by local businessmen in Dunmow, the branch line was first opened in 1869 by the Great Eastern Railway. Over the years more stations were added until around 1922 when a trip from Bishops Stortford to Braintree would take you through Hockrill Halt, Stane Street, Takeley, Easton Lodge, Dunmow, Felsted, Bannister Green and Rayne. This branch ran as a single track and was one of the longest in Essex, running for 18 miles. Easton Lodge station was built for the use of the Earl and Countess of Wessex who agreed to pay £ 52 per year towards the upkeep of the building while also allowing public access. One frequent visitor was the then Prince of Wales who was later to become King Edward VII. During the Second World War the line was often used to supply local airfields including the one at Easton Lodge which was home to the American 386th Bomber Group.

After the war passenger numbers dwindled with growing car and bus use but freight still continued to supply reasonable business. The final passenger service ran in 1952 and freight followed in 1969. Today much of the old branch line has been turned into a public footpath called The Flitch Way and is maintained by Essex County Council. Although some of the station buildings have gone, several are still in place including Rayne station which has been restored to its former glory and can be found on an upcoming walk. Both Bishops Stortford and Braintree are still working stations.

Rayne

Distance: 4 miles
Map: OS Explorer 195 (GR 726225)

Getting there:
Rayne is off the A120 between Little Dunmow and Braintree. Nearest railway station is Braintree.

Parking:
You can park with care on the village streets.

Pubs on route:
The Swan, The Welsh Princess and The Cock are all on Rayne High Street.

Route Map

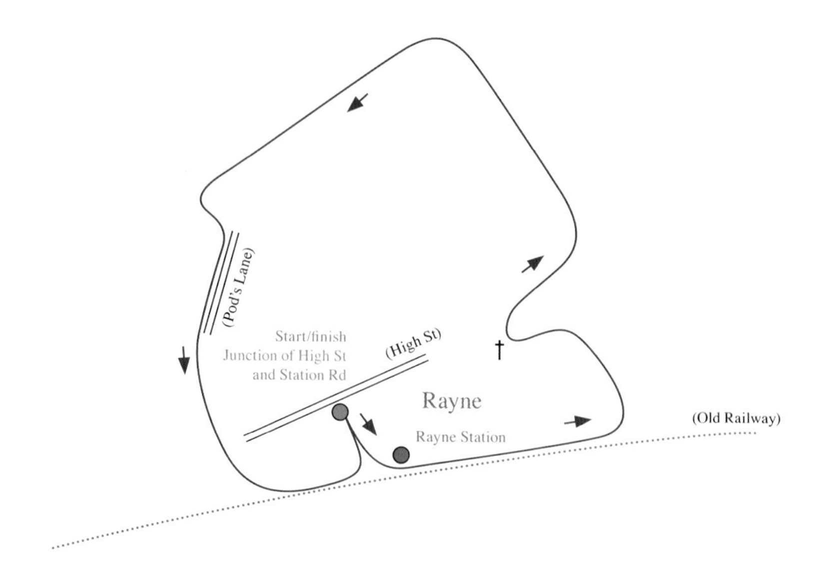

The Walk

This is a short walk starting in Rayne village that takes in some of the old railway that has now become The Flitch Way. Along the way you will visit Rayne station, which has been well restored by Essex County Council and is an excellent example of Victorian railway construction.

Start on the High Street in Rayne at its junction with Station Road. (Along the High Street you have the choice of three pubs to visit either before or after your walk). Turn down Station Road and proceed SA for about 300yds to reach the former Rayne station. (The station buildings have been restored by Essex County Council as part of The Flitch Way and house a small visitor centre and coffee shop. The signal box is now missing but its foundations can still be clearly seen opposite the platform).
Stand on the platform with your back to the station, TL and follow the old track-bed SA with houses on the L until you pass under an old railway bridge (see picture). Continue SA for about 500yds until the railway rises up on an embankment and look out for a FPS on the L (this sign may be missing). TL down the steep embankment for 20yds and then take a sharp R into the field corner and follow the LHFE until you reach the main road (by a house).

TL, cross the road and after 20yds TR at the FPS and go through the hedge into a field. Bear slightly L and then go SA across the field towards the church up ahead and at the field corner follow the LHFE (with church behind the hedge on your L) and after 200yds TL into the churchyard. Go through kissing gate, pass the church on your L and exit onto the main gravel approach road. Follow this road SA and as you reach the green TR across the grass to reach a road (beside a water pump). TR onto the road and immediately TR again down a small lane to pass Rayne Hall Farm on the R. Continue downhill and as the road bottoms out (opposite a pumping station) TL into the field and follow the RHFE beside a stream.

At field corner TR, cross a plank bridge and TL into the next field. Now go SA following the LHFE (stream is now on your L). Again go SA until you reach another plank bridge, TL to cross bridge and follow the RHFE uphill. After 100yds follow the track to the R and cross another plank bridge to reach a small wooded area. TL and continue uphill with a hedge on your L. Eventually the track emerges into a field. Go SA keeping to the LHFE and as the hedge disappears carry on SA. Follow the line of telegraph poles ahead and finally you will reach Pound Farm where you will emerge onto a gravel track. Go SA to reach a FPS by a road and TL.

Follow the lane SA for about 200yds and at the next junction TR down Pods Lane. Follow this lane down to its junction with the main road (Dunmow Road) and go SA across the junction and proceed down Gateswood Lane. After 500yds you will reach the old railway. TL to follow the old track-bed back towards Rayne until you return to the old station building. Finally TL just before the station and walk back up Station Road to its junction with the High St and the end of the walk.

Rayne station possibly in the 1920s (Lens of Sutton)

Rayne Station (2009) is now a visitor centre (author)

All Saints Church (author)

Roadbridge close to Rayne station. Many such bridges still exist on this branch line (author)

Felsted

Distance: 6 - 6½ miles
Map: OS Explorer 195 and 183 (GR 677204)

Getting there:

Felsted is on the B1256 between Little Dunmow and Braintree.

Parking:

There is a public car park next to the church on Station Road. You should also be able to park with care on the quiet side roads in the village.

Pubs on route:

The Swan and the Chequers pubs, Felsted.
The Three Horseshoes, Bannister Green.

Route Map

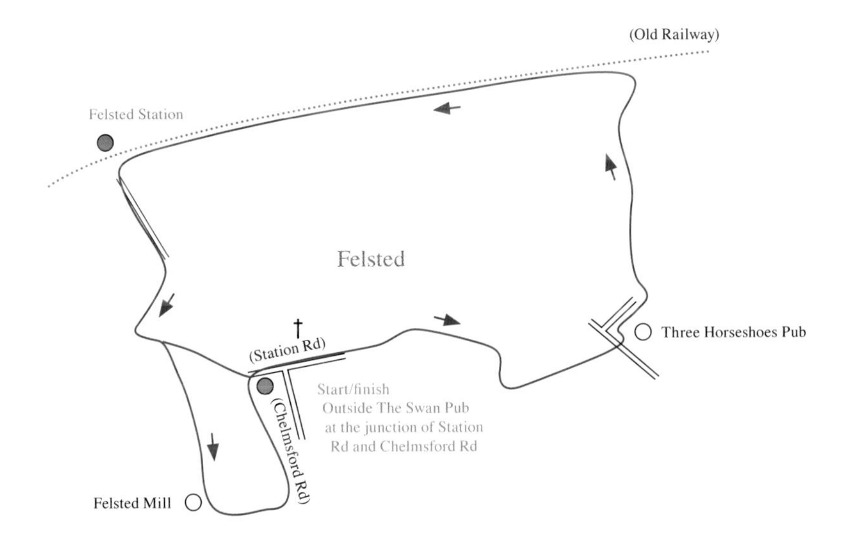

The Walk

Starting in Felsted we head off along Station Road before crossing farmland to reach the old railway for a long walk along The Flitch Way. Then it's a short detour to reach Felsted station before visiting the old watermill and returning to the village.

Start in the centre of Felsted outside the Swan pub at the junction of Station Road and Chelmsford Road. With the pub behind you TR and proceed SA along Station Road (don't go down Chelmsford Road). Along the way you will pass various school buildings on both sides of the road and you will reach the Chequers pub on your L. Continue SA until you pass a playing field on the L, just ahead of you is a bus stop on the R close to a byway sign. TR here and after 50yds TL at FPS to follow a track that passes between houses and continue SA across a field.

At hedge go SA to follow the footpath across the next field and at FPS (by a plank bridge) TR (don't go through the hedge) and follow the LHFE to pass a small wood on L. After 500yds you will reach a FPS, TL and go through the hedge, cross a plank bridge and follow the track that bears L for 50yds and cross another plank bridge through a hedge. Now go SA on a grassy track that leads slightly uphill towards Bannister Green. Go over a stile, cross the next field to a stile in a hedge and then follow the LHFE until the field edge turns sharply L. Now go SA across the field to a FPS by the roadside. At FPS TL onto the road and immediately take the R fork to pass the Three Horseshoes pub.

Just past the pub take the left hand fork in the road and go SA towards the main road ahead. At the junction TL, go SA for 100yds and then TR down Cressages Close. After 100yds TR at FPS and follow the track between the houses and go SA to follow the RHFE. After 300yds you will reach the field corner, continue SA for another 200yds to reach a good track running left to right.

TR along this track and after 50yds TL at FPS and go SA (under electric pylons) to follow the RHFE. TL at field corner and after 50yds TR at FPS and go SA across the field to reach the old railway formation. Now TL for a long walk along the old track-bed. (This is The Flitch Way).

After about ½ mile you will pass under a bridge (although nothing now remains this was the site of the former Bannister Green Halt). Follow the old railway SA for another long walk and you will eventually cross over an old iron bridge (see picture). Continue SA until you reach a break in the railway (at this point the bridge over Station Road has been dismantled) and on reaching the road TR for 100yds (pass the bridge) TL at the FPS, and go up the steps to find the old Felsted station building, which is now a private house.

Now retrace your steps, go back onto the road (past the bridge again) and proceed SA along Station Road. Carry on downhill until you cross a river. Follow the road SA to return to Felsted and at the next road junction you have a choice: go SA back into the village and the end of your walk, or TR to follow this country lane down to visit Felsted Water Mill (see below).

To visit the Mill simply TR to follow the lane downhill and after 500yds you will reach the Water Mill. Opposite the Mill (on the other side of the road) you will find a FPS. TR and proceed SA into a field and follow the RHFE on a good track uphill. At the top corner of the field bear round to the L and TR after 20yds and follow the RHFE with a good hedge on your R. At field corner TL and continue along the RHFE back towards Felsted. Finally emerge onto a dirt track (beside the allotments) and continue SA into the village and the end of your walk.

Felsted station under the GER in the early 1900s (Lens of Sutton)

Felsted station (front view) in 2009 (author)

The iron railway bridge still present on The Flitch Way (author)

Felsted Watermill (author)

Little Easton and Easton Lodge

Distance: 6¾ miles

Map: OS Explorer 195 (GR 608242)

Getting there:

Little Easton is situated off the B184 just north of Great Dunmow

Parking:

You will be able to park with consideration on the streets of the village

Pubs on route:

The Stag pub is in Little Easton.

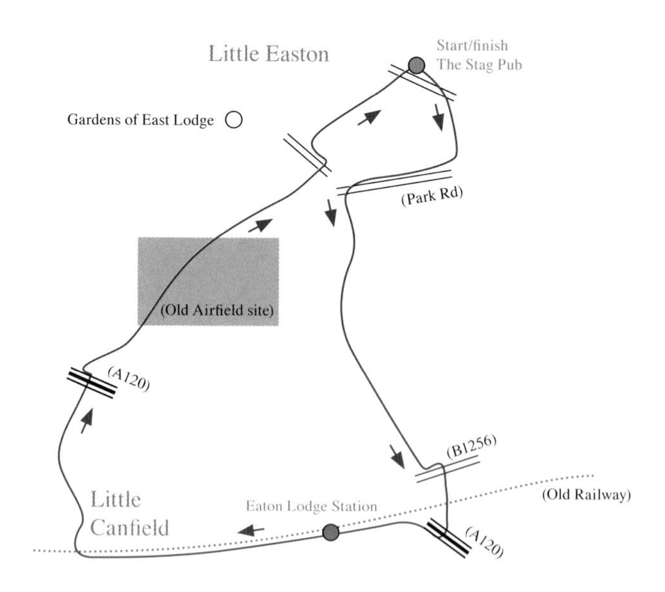

The Walk

Starting and finishing in the village of Little Easton this walk takes us down to the old station of Easton Lodge before a good walk along the old track-bed to finally return via Little Canfield and the site of the old Easton Airfield.

Start at The Stag pub in Little Easton village. With the pub behind you TL and follow the main road through the village for about 300yds. Cross the road to find a FPS beside some houses (note there are two signposts here) and take the LH footpath sign to follow the track between the houses for 50yds to bring you to a field. Continue SA following a line of trees ahead to walk uphill. Eventually you will reach a house by a road. Follow the track round to the L of the house and on reaching the road TR and carry on SA to reach Little Easton Church. Immediately after the church TL at a FPS and follow the track to the L of the lake to bring you into a field.

Now proceed SA following the RHFE for a long walk gently uphill. As the ground levels out the area to your R will become more wooded until you pass under a pylon. Go SA across the next field and when you reach the field corner go SA into the next field following the RHFE with a wood on your R. On reaching a main road TL for 100yds and then TR down a small dead-end lane to pass Highwood Farm on your R. After another 100yds cross the old railway formation (don't go onto the railway yet) and continue SA towards the busy A120 dual carriageway.

Cross the road using the bridge and immediately TR at the FPS to follow the track as it runs parallel to the road. After 300yds you can pick up the old railway formation and continue SA to follow the old track-bed. Soon you will reach the old Easton Lodge Station building, which is now a private house. The station was opened in 1894 and was constructed for the use of the Earl and Countess of Warwick who lived nearby at Easton Lodge.

The Countess paid an annual fee towards the upkeep of the site and in return the station was also open for public use. The station closed in 1952. The wooden hut, which is still present in the front garden of the house, originally housed the levers for the level crossing. Now walk along the road with the station on your L and after 50yds TL onto a footpath, which will bring you behind the house and back onto the railway formation. Continue SA for a long walk along the old railway.

Eventually you will reach some wooden steps that will bring you up onto a road (the original bridge is still there but has been filled in with earth). TR onto the road for 50yds and then TL down some more steps to bring you back to the railway where you should carry on SA. Immediately after crossing an old metal bridge TL to follow a track down the embankment to reach a lane. Go under the bridge and follow this lane SA for 200yds to reach a main road junction. Now cross the main road to reach a FPS and follow the narrow lane ahead towards Canfield Hall. Follow the road that passes to the L of the Hall and then continue SA on a dirt track for 50yds (passing a garden on your R) to finally reach a grass footpath. Bear R and head for the A120 footbridge up ahead.

Having crossed the A120 ignore the first FPS that you come to and instead follow the grassy track that bears slightly R to proceed uphill. At the field edge (by a metal gate) you should see a 'permissive access' signpost. TL here and follow the RHFE to eventually head downhill to the field corner.

Now TR and head uphill to another FPS by a tarmac track. Go SA across the next field, cross another tarmac road and follow the footpath across the next field. (This large, flat area of countryside was once the former Easton Lodge Airfield. From here American bombers launched attacks into Europe during World War Two. Some of the concrete roads that you are crossing at this point were part of the original airfield construction).

When you reach the junction of several concrete roads follow the bridleway sign that points SA across the next field (towards a wood). Finally you will reach a road (with a pond on your R). TL and follow the road SA for 200yds to reach a junction. *(If you go SA at this junction you can visit the Garden of Easton Lodge).

At the junction TR at the FPS onto a good track and proceed SA for the walk back to Little Easton. As you come into the village you will pass a cricket pitch on your L. Continue SA for 300yds to reach a road junction where you will find yourself back at The Stag pub and the end of your walk.

*The Gardens of Easton Lodge
For further information and opening times:

www.eastonlodge.co.uk
Tel: 01371 876 979

The station under GER ownership in the early 1900s (Lens of Sutton)

Easton Lodge (front view) 2009. The platform has gone but the wooden hut which contained the level crossing levers is still present (author)

Takeley and Hatfield Forest

Distance: 6¾ miles
Map: OS Explorer 195 and 183 (GR 524204)

Getting there:

The Sir John Houblon pub is situated off the B1256 Dunmow Road and is close to Great Hallingbury. Come off the M11 at junction 8, follow signs for Takeley and then head for Great Hallingbury.

Parking:

You should be able to park opposite the pub or along the lane nearby

Pubs on route:

The Sir John Houblon, (formerly The Hop Poles) near Great Hallingbury. The Four Ashes in Takeley. The Visitor Centre at Hatfield Forest also sells hot and cold refreshments during opening hours.

Route Map

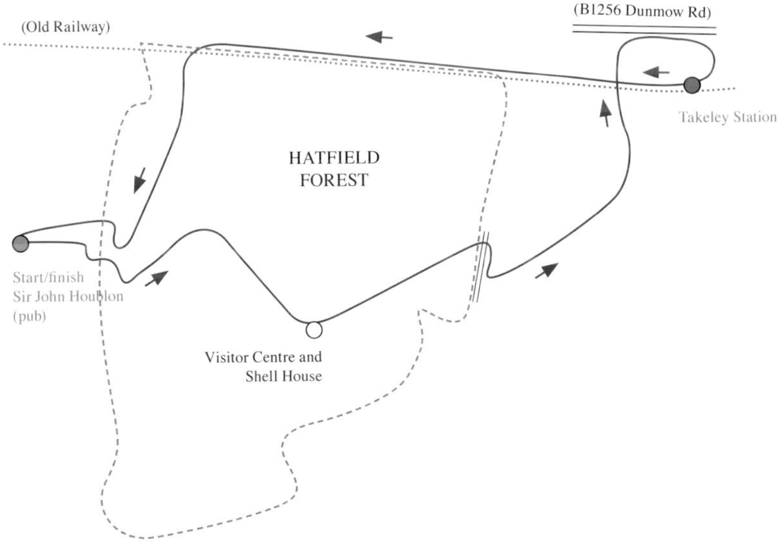

The Walk

A great walk that takes in a long stretch of the old Bishops Stortford to Braintree Railway. Along the way you can visit the former station at Takeley as well as enjoy ancient Hatfield Forest.

Start at the Sir John Houblon pub near Great Hallingbury. Walk down the narrow lane (away from the main road) and pass the pub on your L. Follow the right hand FPS and go SA down the narrow lane that leads to Beggars Hall. Follow the road past the hall and on reaching farm buildings, look for a gate leading into the forest ahead. Once through the gate TR and follow the grassy track SA for about 200yds. Where the track forks, bear L and carry on SA on a wide grass track bordered by trees on both sides.

After another 200yds you will come to a much wider clearing. Go SA along this 'avenue' for about 500yds until you reach a National Trust signpost. (Most of the FPS within Hatfield Forest are of the National Trust style; this is a white disk with black lettering). TR at this signpost and follow the track ahead. Look out for the signposts which are dotted across the wide common ahead until you finally reach a road. Continue SA along this road until you reach the Visitor Centre.

Follow the path past the Centre and down to the lake. Now TR (picking up the National Trust signposts again) pass the Shell House on your R, and follow the path round the lake. On leaving the lake the path now become timbered. Follow this timbered path SA through the wood until you reach a tarmac road. TR onto the road and carry on SA for 300yds to reach a cattle grid and a car park. Now exit the forest onto the main road, TR and proceed SA to pass a church on your L. Just after the church TL at a road junction (signposted Bush End) and continue for 500yds.

TL at FPS (by a bend in the road and opposite a house) go over a stile and proceed across the field ahead.

At field corner go SA following the LHFE for 100yds then TL at FPS and immediately bear R to follow an enclosed track to cross a stream using a plank bridge. Continue SA and follow the RHFE for a long walk until you reach the field corner. Go SA into the next field and once again follow the RHFE.

At the next field corner proceed SA to go through a hedge to reach the old railway formation. Now cross over the railway and carry on SA on an enclosed track for 200yds until you reach a main road (Dunmow Road). TR and follow the road through Takeley until you reach a set of traffic lights. TR at the lights (The Four Ashes pub is on the corner here) and after 50yds TL down Elm Close. Immediately TR along Sycamore Close and after 100yds you will reach the old Takeley station house. Takeley station (1869-1952) is now a private house.

Now stand on the platform with your back to the station, TR and follow the old railway formation as it goes under the bridge. You will now take a long walk along the old track-bed which has been designated part of The Flitch Way country park. Pass the sewage works on your L and then cross an old iron bridge to eventually walk along the northern edge of Hatfield Forest. As you proceed SA you will pass through several 'five bar' wooden gates and eventually come to a gate on the L with signage for both Hatfield Forest and a walk called the 3 Forest Way.

TL through this gate and go SA bearing slightly R to cross a clearing in the woods. (Be careful here, some of the footpaths are indistinct. You should be heading SA and slightly to the R). Eventually you will reach a wide clearing (or avenue) running left to right in front of you. TR to follow this wide grassy track and after 300yds TR down a narrower track to reach a red brick farm building (Beggars Hall). Stay in the forest and TR before you reach the red brick building and follow the track away from the hall for 300yds. TL at a stile and follow the LHFE to reach the field corner. Finally proceed SA onto a wide track, which will bring you back to The Sir John Houblon pub.

Takeley station 1958 (P Paye)

The station in 2009 (author)

Sir John Houblon pub, (formerly known as The Hop Poles) at the start and finish of the walk (author)

Old iron railway bridge at Little Canfield (author)

Elsenham to Thaxted Light Railway

Built to provide a much-needed lifeline to rural Thaxted, construction of the railway started in 1911 and the line opened on 31st March 1913. The railway gained the nickname the 'Gin and Toffee Line' after the prominent local businessmen William Gilby (a wine merchant) and George Lee (the Thaxted sweet maker) who both had great influence in the original construction. Apart from the stations at Thaxted and Sibleys three intermediate halts were built at Mill Road, Henham and Cutlers Green. These were often low-key constructions with a simple raised clinker platform and waiting rooms fashioned from old railway carriages. This single track railway performed a simple push-pull service up to six times a day in each direction at a top speed of 25mph, slowing to 10mph when approaching the ungated level crossings. On board the train tickets were issued by the guard with only one class of travel offered.

Despite a plan to extend the line through to Great Bardfield, the railway never saw large passenger numbers during its life and services were cutback during the Second World War. The original decision to build Thaxted station one mile short of the village (to avoid the cost of building a viaduct to cross the Chelmer Valley) now hampered its usefulness to passengers and made it hard to compete with the new bus and coach services. The final passenger train ran in 1952 and the line closed completely a year later.

Due to its Light Railway construction little remains today of the Elsenham to Thaxted railway. A few raised embankments still exist but all the stations have long gone. All that is except Thaxted itself; where the original brick engine shed can still be seen along with some of the old platform buildings. Elsenham is still a working station.

Thaxted

Distance: 6½ miles
Map: OS Explorer 195 (GR 611311)

Getting there:

Thaxted is on the B184 south of Saffron Walden. It can be accessed from Junction 8a of the M11, follow the A120 and head for Great Dunmow.

Parking:

There are several pay and display car parks in Thaxted.

Food and drink on route:

The Star Inn and The Rose and Crown Inn are both in Thaxted. The Farmhouse Inn, off the Dunmow Rd. There are also various tea shops and restaurants in the town.

Route Map

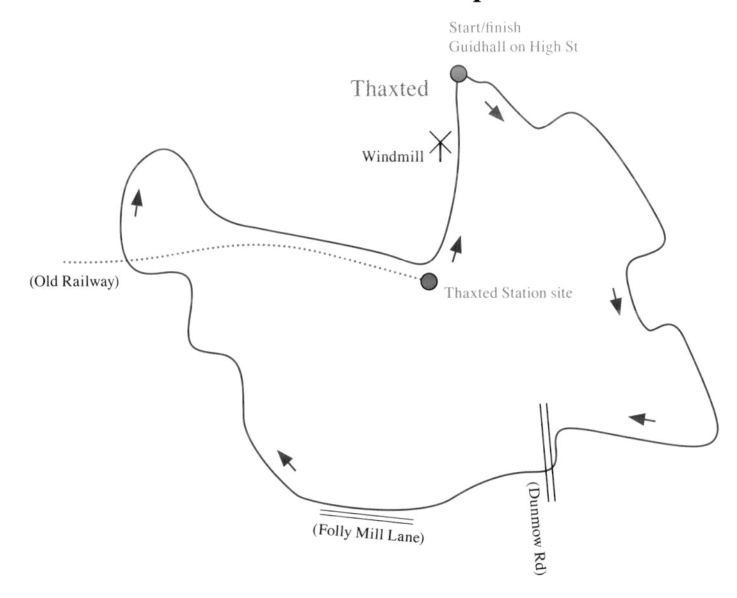

The Walk

Starting in one of the oldest towns in Essex the walk takes in some great views along the Chelmer Valley before passing the old Thaxted station site to finally return to town via the Windmill. Although there is very little left of this Light Railway the route of the walk is so good that it justifies being included in the book.

Start at the Guildhall on the High Street (behind the church). With the Guildhall behind you go SA down the High Street passing the Post Office on your L. Stay on the main road to pass first the Star Inn, and then a garage on your R. After the garage TL at the road junction onto Bardfield Road and go SA passing the Fire Station on the R.

After 200yds TR at FPS and follow the good track SA to a row of trees up ahead. Continue SA passing to the L of the trees to follow the track between fields to eventually head uphill and reach a FPS at the top corner of the field. Now TR and follow the LHFE until you finally head downhill between fields to reach a FPS in the middle of the field. (This is the junction of several footpaths). TL and follow the track uphill towards a hedgerow and follow the field edge to the field corner. TL at FPS and follow LHFE for 100yds to another FPS where you should TR and follow the track towards Richmonds Farm. Follow the path SA through the farm and finally bear R onto a small road and go SA to reach a road junction 200yds ahead.

Go SA on this country lane as it eventually heads downhill to a main road junction. (There are some fine views along here). At the junction TL onto the Dunmow Road and proceed SA, keeping to the verge. After 400yds you will reach a junction, TR down the lane and pass the Farmhouse Inn on your L. Continue SA for 200yds and then TR down Folly Mill Lane. Now follow this very quite lane as it passes down into the Chelmer Valley and up the other side. (More good views here). On reaching a road junction go SA onto the road opposite to pass a lake on the L.

Eventually you will reach another junction where you should go SA onto a good enclosed track to follow the footpath uphill. At the highest point cross the fields ahead to reach a FPS. TR to follow a dirt track downhill to pass Browns Wood on your L. As the wood ends follow the dirt road round to the R, then immediately TL into a field and keep to the LHFE to find a FPS 50yds ahead. Follow this good track SA (the old railway followed the hedgerow on your L). When you reach a good dirt track TR towards the Water Tower. Cutlers Green Halt stood at this junction (see picture). The station must have been one of the most remote in Essex. Sadly nothing now remains.

After passing the tower go SA past Loves Farm to reach a road. Continue on this road through the small hamlet of Cutlers Green for about 500yds to reach a FPS on the R. Now go SA on this enclosed track to reach a field ahead, follow LHFE, cross into another field and again keep to LHFE and eventually you will begin to head downhill with Thaxted over to your L. As you reach the bottom of the hill follow the concrete road ahead. (What remains of Thaxted station is now in the industrial park on the R. The engine shed and water tower are clearly visible from the footpath and the old green waiting room with pitched roof can be seen further down).

Follow the road to reach a metal gate and bear L onto the grass verge. TL to follow the road ahead for 200yds. At FPS TL and follow the RHFE towards the windmill and church ahead. Pass the Windmill and continue SA to return to Thaxted via the back streets.

The former halt at Cutlers Green (P Paye)

View on the approach to Thaxted (author)

Thaxted Windmill (author)

Thaxted engine shed and water tower in 2010 (author). Built in 1913 this is the only surviving building of its kind in Essex

The Saffron Walden Railway

By the early 1860s the town of Saffron Walden was thriving, with its cultivation of the saffron crocus plus the growing businesses of malting and brewing. Add to this the town's proximity to the Liverpool Street to Cambridge main line and it is no wonder that many people thought the town deserving of its own railway. However the Eastern Counties Railway (ECR) didn't agree and it was eventually local money that created the independent Saffron Walden Railway in 1865. Initially the line only ran from Audley End to Saffron Walden but a further extension in 1866 took it via Ashdon Halt to Bartlow where it met the Stour Valley line.

The branch was always in financial difficulty and eventually it was bought in 1877 by the ECR. Passenger numbers were reasonable through the 1940s with even daily through trains to London and a new stop (Acrow Halt) added in 1957 to service the new engineering works. However, from then on numbers declined and even the introduction of diesel railbuses in 1958 couldn't stop the rot. Dr Beeching earmarked the line for closure and passenger services stopped in 1964, with freight following soon after.

The line today has disappeared in places, particularly around Saffron Walden. However, Ashdon halt still boasts its clinker platform and old railway carriage cum waiting room, while at Bartlow the frame of the old signal box can still be seen. Audley End is still a working station and the old Saffron Walden branch waiting room is still present. At Saffron Walden the old station building is now a private house while the old Station pub is still open and worth a visit.

Saffron Walden

Distance: 4 miles
Map: OS Explorer 195 (GR 539380)

Getting there:

Saffron Walden is on the B184 and can be accessed from J9 of the M11. Nearest railway station is Audley End. The old railway station is on Station Road

Parking:

There are several pay and display car parks in the town centre

Pubs on route:

The Railway pub, The Temeraire and The Duke of York are all in Saffron Walden

Route Map

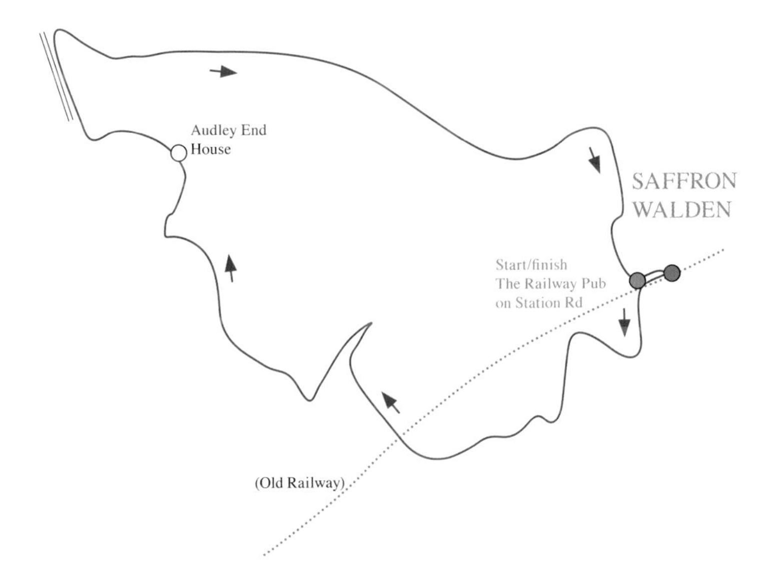

The Walk

Starting at the Railway pub we visit the old Saffron Walden station before leaving town to travel cross country to the historic Audley End House and Gardens. Then it's a long walk back with a chance to stop off in town to see the local sights.

Start at the Station pub on Station Road. With your back to the pub TL up Station Road to visit the old Saffron Walden Station building 100yds down on the R. (The white brick building was built in 1865 and has been renovated with some care). Now turn back up Station Road and pass the pub on your R. (The Station pub is well worth a visit as it has lots of railway memorabilia, old posters and interesting photographs, relating to the Saffron Walden Railway). Now go SA to the end of the road and TL onto the main road, cross over the old railway bridge and head uphill. Take the next right turn (Borough Lane), and follow the road round to reach Springhill Road.

TL and follow this road to the end. Now TR onto Summerhill Road and at its junction with the main road ahead TL. After 100yds TR onto Beeches Close and go SA. Follow the road as it finally bears L and look for FPS on the R. TR and follow the path between the houses to reach an enclosed track (the old railway embankment is on your R). Eventually the track takes a sharp right turn. (Here the railway followed the line of telegraph poles across the fields on the L towards Audley End Station). Now follow the track SA until you finally reach a road.

TL to follow the road downhill and after 400yds TR at FPS to follow a tarmac road SA. Pass farm buildings on your L and finally a row of whitewashed cottages to reach a main road. TL and after 200yds you will reach Audley End House. (On the left is the miniature railway which is open at weekends from March to October). If you are not going into the house then follow the main road SA to cross a bridge over the lake.

Continue to the junction and take the R fork and proceed SA with the gardens on your R. (If you are going into the house make sure that you exit by following the approach road to leave the gardens at the gate house by the cricket pitch). Once back on the main road stay on the footpath with the walled garden on you R and look for a FPS on the L by a house, and TR down a good track, (signposted Home Farm). Now go SA with fields on your L, pass over a small stream and as road bears L go SA down an enclosed track.

When you emerge into a field continue SA following the LHFE. A golf course and stream should be on your L. After a long walk cross a stream using a plank bridge and go SA across the next field. TL at house on L, go through a gate and proceed SA on road ahead to bring you back into Saffron Walden. On reaching the main road junction TR into the High Street, pass the pub, The Temeraire, on your R and continue SA uphill. At the next junction follow the road that bears to the R, pass the Duke of York pub and then TL down Debden Road. After 200yds TL down Station Road and you will be back at The Railway pub and the end of the walk.

An early view of Saffron Walden station (top right) NRM Collection

Saffron Walden station building, now a private house (author)

One of many charming side streets in the town (author)

Ashdon to Bartlow

Distance: 7½ miles
Map: OS Explorer 209

Getting there:
M11 to junction 9, then A11 to the A1307 (Cambridge Rd) and look for signs to Bartlow and Ashdon

Parking:
You can park with consideration in the village

Pubs on route:
The Rose and Crown, Ashdon
The Three Hills, Bartlow

Route Map

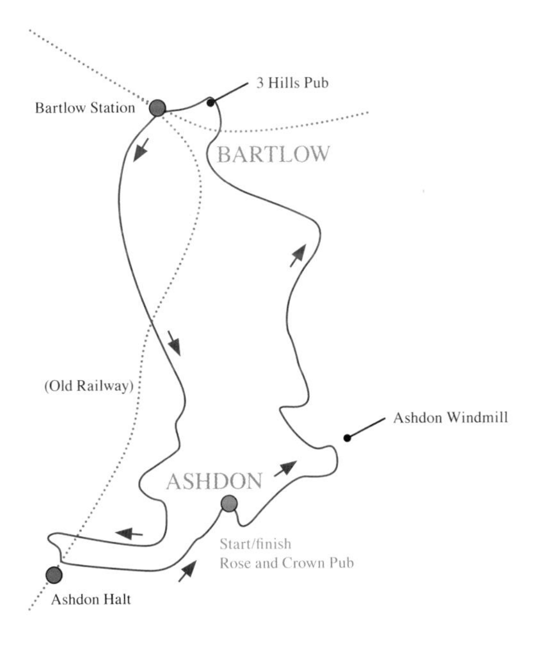

The Walk

The longest walk in the book takes you via Ashdon Windmill to Bartlow in Cambridgeshire where you can see the ancient Bartlow Hills burial mounds, before stopping off at the local pub. Then we pick up the old railway at Bartlow station before heading back cross country to see Ashdon halt, finally returning to the village and the Rose and Crown pub.

Start outside the Rose and Crown pub in Ashdon. With the pub behind you go SA down the road opposite, passing the White Horse House and Village Hall on your R. After passing the Baptist Church on your L, TL up Kates Lane. After 200yds TL at FPS to follow a good track to the top of the hill keeping to LHFE and at field corner go SA, through hedge into next field and proceed SA keeping once more to the LHFE. At field corner TL at FPS and go SA into next field keeping to RHFE (windmill is ahead). Pass Ashdon Windmill to find a small road behind. TL, away from the cottages, and follow the road downhill.

At main road junction TR for 300yds to find a FPS on L. TL and follow the road round to the L (passing Ashdon Hall on R) and continue SA on a good track through mature trees. As track bears L go SA at FPS keeping to RHFE. As hedgerow ends go SA across field to eventually follow the track uphill. On reaching a wide dirt track TL and keep to the RHFE to follow this good track downhill. Just before reaching the main road TR to pass Hills Farm on your R and the circular grain store on L. Follow the track downhill and TR at FPS, go up steps and through a small wood. Just before a sharp R turn on the footpath, exit onto the main road to see the old Bartlow station building (now called the Old Booking Hall) up ahead.

Now return to the footpath and follow it SA to reach Bartlow Hills. In the far corner, behind one of the mounds, follow the footpath as it crosses a brick railway bridge (part of the old branch line to Sudbury). You should now be on an enclosed track, sometimes fenced on both sides, finally to cross a small stream to reach Bartlow Church.Bear R to pass the church and follow the path to reach the main entrance gate. Now TL onto the main road and after 200yds TL at the next road junction to bring you to the Three Hills pub.

With the pub behind you TL onto the main road and after 300yds TR at the road junction, signposted to Hadstock. (The tree line on your L marks the route of the Sudbury branch). Continue on this road to pass under the old demolished railway bridge and immediately TL up a dirt track. If you wish to explore what remains of Bartlow station bear L and behind the mounds of earth you will find the wooden frame of the old signal box. Further behind is the overgrown platform and in the field behind that is the former Bartlow station building; now a private house. (Bartlow was the junction of two lines: The Saffron Walden Railway and the Sudbury to Shelford branch line).

Now go back to the road and continue away from Bartlow, towards a FPS up ahead on the L. TL and follow this track. When you reach a fork in this track bear L (don't go towards the woods ahead) and go SA on this good dirt track. Just past a bridleway sign you will see a house on your L. The railway passed behind the house following the tree line to go under the footpath at the railway bridge ahead. Go over the bridge and follow the track as it bears L. About 100yds before the sewage works TR at FPS, go through hedge and follow the LHFE beside a river. Go over a stile and proceed SA into next field staying with the LHFE. At the field corner cross stile and turn sharp R onto the road towards the farm ahead.

As you reach the farmhouse on right, TL, pass farm building on your R to finally bear R to pass behind the farm and head for a small bridge hidden in the hedge (behind a tyre dump). Cross stile into field and keep to RHFE. At field corner TL and follow the hedge uphill to a stile. TL onto road and go SA to pass a house on L. TR at FPS and cross field, go through a gate and follow track ahead. As you reach a row of telegraph poles TR and follow the track SA across field.

Now cross several stiles to reach a road. Go SA across road to reach another stile hidden in the hedge. Follow RHFE and at bottom corner of field exit to FPS on a gatepost. Bear L and follow track SA (telegraph poles ahead). On reaching a lane TR for 200yds to reach the remains of Ashdon halt.

Now turn around and retrace your steps back down the lane towards Ashdon village. At the main road junction TL and follow the road for 100yds to reach a tarmac footpath that runs parallel to the main road. Now proceed SA to head downhill until you reach Ashdon Museum.* Finally, continue on this road back into the village and the Rose and Crown pub to finish your walk.

*Ashdon Museum is well worth a visit as it contains a large collection of photographs and memorabilia from the village and surrounding countryside throughout the ages. It has limited opening times. For more information call: 01799 584253

Bartlow Junction 1911. The Saffron Walden branch is in the foreground (NRM Collection)

An excellent view of Bartlow in 1911 showing the burial mounds in the background, Station house and Sudbury Branch to the left, and Saffron Walden Branch, (with waiting room) on the right. (NRM Collection)

Ashdon Windmill (author)

Ashdon halt in the 1950s (Courtesy of Ashdon Museum)

The same view in 2009, note the waiting room is still present (author)

Chappel to Haverhill (The Colne Valley Railway)

The independent Colne Valley and Halstead Railway (CVHR) opened the line from Chappel to Halstead in 1860 and then a further extension was made to Haverhill in 1863. The railway ran for 13 miles with stations at Chappel and Wakes Colne, White Colne, Earls Colne, Halstead, Sible and Castle Headingham, Yeldham, Birdbrook and Haverhill. The railway had an uneasy relationship with the Eastern Counties Railway which ran the Marks Tey to Sudbury branch line, and who saw them as competition to their own Stour Valley railway. However, the CVHR eventually became part of the LNER in 1923.

The branch line had reasonable passenger numbers both before and after the First World War. However, World War Two saw the railway switch to providing troop movements and munition supplies to the local airfields which obviously affected ordinary passenger numbers. The 1950s Modernisation Plan saw diesel replacing steam on the line, but this did not stop the branch losing out to other forms of transport and the last passenger service ran in December in 1961 with freight following in 1965.

Today many of the railway structures still survive on the Chappel to Haverhill line. Chappel and Wakes Colne (still a working station) is now home to the East Anglian Railway Museum while further down the line Sible and Castle Headingham station now hosts the Colne Valley Railway Preservation Society. Both have working steam engines and a great collection of memoribillia, and both can be found in walks in this book. There are also several station buildings present at both White Colne and Earls Colne and let's not forget the magnificent 32 arch viaduct at Chappel, also to be found on an upcoming walk.

Chappel to White Colne

Distance: 6½ miles
Map: OS Explorer 195 (GR 895284)

Getting there:

Chappel and Wakes Colne railway station in on the branch line from Marks Tey to Sudbury. By car Chappel is on the A1124 between Colchester and Halstead

Parking:

You should be able to use the car park at the railway station

Food and drink on the route:

The Swan Inn, Chappel

Route Map

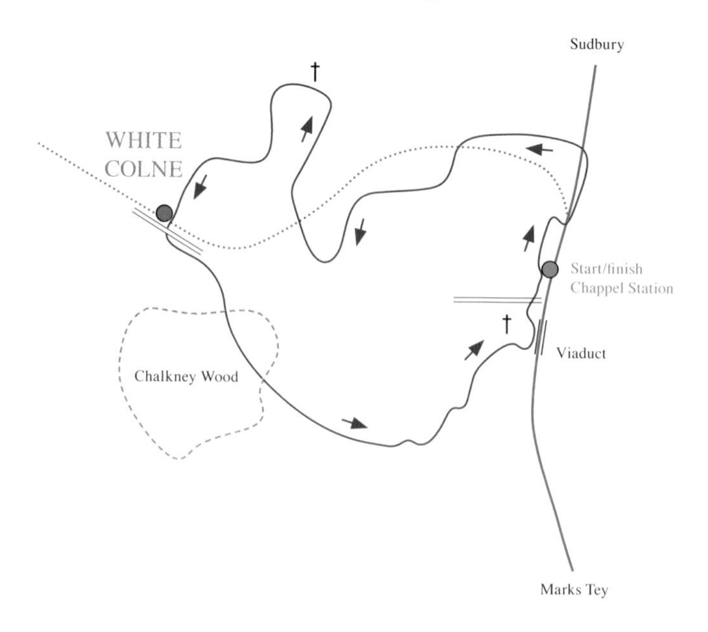

The Walk

A great walk that starts and finishes at Chappel and Wakes Colne station. Along the way you will visit the former station at White Colne and take in some spectacular views along the Colne Valley before arriving at the Chappel Viaduct. All of this plus the East Anglian Railway Museum.

Start at Chappel station. Stand with your back to the station and TL down the approach road to reach the main road junction. TR onto Bures Road and continue SA for about 400yds (watch out for traffic here). At the road junction TR down Spring Gardens Road and cross the railway bridge. (Look to your L over the bridge; this is where the Halstead branch used to curve in to meet the Sudbury Line). Just after the bridge TL at FPS and follow the LHFE beside the railway, go through a hedge and continue along the LHFE of the next field. At the field corner go through the hedge into a wood and immediately bear L to follow the footpath close to the railway. After about 200yds look for a FPS and take a sharp L to follow a path leading down to the railway crossing gate. (This is close to the corner of the wood). Cross the railway (watching out for trains) and go over a plank bridge into a field.

Now go SA across the field towards the road ahead. On reaching the road go SA (bear very slightly L) to find a FPS hidden in the hedge opposite, and follow the path SA to pass to the L of a house. Follow the track behind the house and as the house ends TL to proceed SA on a path that follows a line of telegraph poles ahead. Follow the RHFE ahead, go through a hedge to a FPS and then go SA across the next field (passing a large tree in the middle). You are heading for a FPS under a telegraph pole on your R. At this FPS go SA along LHFE for 100yds to reach a road.

TL and follow the road SA (passing farm buildings) as the road rises up to pass over the old railway bridge. After 300yds TR at FPS and follow the track ahead across the field towards a wood.

Follow the path as it passes to the L of the wood and walk downhill to follow the RHFE. (The tree line to your far R is the old railway embankment). Exit field at a FPS on your R and go SA through a field of birch trees. Now cross a stile and go SA along the RHFE to reach the main road ahead. TR onto the road and go SA for 200yds to reach a small lane on the R (Boley Road). TR up this lane to head uphill. At the brow of the hill is where the railway used to cross the road at a level crossing.

Pass down the other side of the hill and take a long walk along this quiet lane. Follow the road as it bears round to the L to eventually pass St Andrews Church on your L. Continue SA for another 200yds to reach a FPS on the L. Follow the track SA across the field (following a row of trees) and cross a plank bridge to reach a FPS hidden in the hedge. TR keeping to the RHFE to eventually reach a road. TL and follow the road towards White Colne. Just before arriving at a main road junction TR to find the former White Colne Station building which has now become the Village Hall. (There used to be a level crossing here and the station platform was on the opposite side of the road, where new houses are sited).

Now go down to the road junction and TL (towards Colchester) and proceed SA for about 600yds to reach a FPS on the R. TR down this good tarmac road (towards Chalkney Mill and Kennels) and pass a lake on your L. Bear L under the pylon to follow the road towards the weather-boarded mill ahead. After passing the mill go SA passing the kennels and head into Chalkney Wood. Carry on uphill on a good dirt track keeping L where possible and when you finally exit the woods follow the path ahead to reach a road. TR onto the road and after 20yds TL at a FPS (beside a cottage). Now follow this enclosed track SA and cross a plank bridge to reach a field. Now go SA uphill, through gate and across the next field following the LHFE. Pass a lake on your R and aim for the woods ahead. Go SA through the woods to exit into a field. Continue SA following the LHFE and follow the footpath round to exit onto a road.

TL and follow the road SA (you should be able to see Chappel Viaduct soon) and as the road bends to the R look for a FPS on the L (pointing towards a church). Follow this track across the field ahead (look out for sheep) and at FPS TR to follow the LHFE down to the field corner. Go through kissing gate on L and then follow the RHFE for 100yds to reach a road. TL and follow this road into Chappel. On your L is St Barnabas Church. Opposite the church is a gravel track, go SA towards the viaduct and when you reach it TL to follow the path SA (passing children's playground on L). After 100yds go through a gate on the L to bring you to the rear of the Swan Inn.

Pass the Inn on your L and exit onto the road. TR and go to the junction ahead. Finally cross the junction and go SA along Station Road, which takes you uphill where you will find Chappel and Wakes Colne station on the right.

Don't forget to visit the Railway Museum during your walk. It has a good display of railway memorabilia and working trains as well as running special theme days throughout the year.

For more information go to: www.earm.co.uk

Chappel in the 1950s (NRM Collection)

The station exterior (2009) has changed very little over the years (author)

White Colne in the 1940s

White Colne today. Although the platform and level crossings have been removed the Station building remains as a village hall. Note the tall chimney pots visible in both photographs (author)

The splendid 32 arch Chappel Viaduct looms over the end of your walk and is the largest railway structure in Essex (author)

The Swan Inn at Chappel has a reputation for good food (author)

Earls Colne

Distance: 6½ miles
Map: OS Explorer 195 (GR 856289)

Getting there:

Earls Colne is on the A1124 between Halstead and White Colne. The nearest railway station in at Chappel and Wakes Colne

Parking:

There is a public car par off the High Street at its junction with Queens Road

Food and drink on route:

The Drum Inn and the Lion pub in Earls Colne. The Five Bells pub in Colne Engaine

Route Map

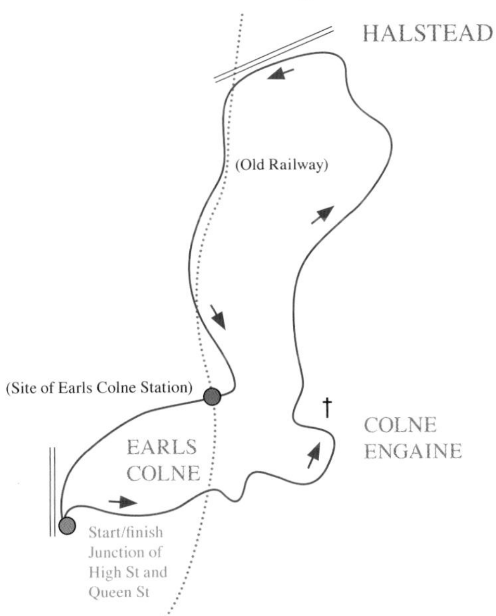

The Walk

Leaving the town we head out towards Halstead via Colne Engaine along quiet country lanes before following the old railway back along the valley to the site of Earls Colne station. All this plus three pubs en-route.

Start in the town of Earls Colne at the junction of Queens Road and the High Street (convenience store is on the corner). With your back to Queens Road TR and proceed SA along the High Street passing first The Drum Inn and then the Lion pub. After 50yds TR down Burrows Road and go SA to the road junction. Continue SA along a dead-end road to reach a FPS at a stile. Follow the track SA (don't go to the R) onto an enclosed track to reach a golf course. Go SA across the course (path is hard to find) bearing slightly L and go downhill into the Colne Valley.

At the bottom of the valley pass a lake and bear L to reach a footbridge to cross the River Colne. Immediately after the bridge go SA to cross the old railway embankment ahead, then bear L to follow the grassy track beside the river for 50yds. Now TR to follow an enclosed track uphill towards farm buildings. On reaching a road TL and go SA (good views of the Colne Valley here) for 200yds to reach a FPS on the R. Go SA following the RHFE until you enter the next field and then follow the LHFE to reach the field corner. TL to follow a good track towards the village of Colne Engaine.

On reaching a road (opposite school) TL into the village and follow the road downhill as it bears L, pass the village shop and keep L to finally reach the Five Bells pub. Now turn around and with the pub behind you TR to find a FPS (beside a phone box) and follow the path up to St Andrews Church. Pass the church on your R to exit at the front gates onto a road junction. Go SA along Brook Street to follow the road out of the village. Now take a long walk along this quiet country lane and ignore any minor side roads that you will come across.

After half a mile or more you will pass a small nursery hidden on your left quickly followed by a collection of cottages. The road begins to head downhill just after a large house on the R called Abbot Shrubs and you should see the town of Halstead spread out in the distance. As you reach the outskirts of the town the road meets a T junction. TL onto Fenn Road and go SA (passing an ambulance station on the L) to reach a mini roundabout. Now TL to follow the main road downhill for 500yds to eventually pass the Bluebridge Industrial Estate on the L. Stay on the main road for 50yds to reach a dismantled railway bridge.

Climb the steep embankment on the L, cross over the railway and drop down the other side to bring you into a field. Turn sharp L and follow the LHFE, keeping the old railway on your L for a long walk. Follow this track SA along the Colne Valley beside the railway until you eventually exit onto a road with a house (Langley Mill) on your R. (The track may be slightly indistinct as you approach the mill). On reaching the road follow it SA, (it bears round to the L as the old railway formation goes straight across the road) and you will immediately reach a road junction. Take the R fork that heads towards Colne Engaine and follow this quiet lane as it passes several detached houses along the valley. (You may see the old railway embankment over to the R).

After around half a mile you will come to a main road junction. TR and go SA towards Earls Colne, cross over the river at the bridge, and after 100yds you will come to the former Earls Colne station site. (This substantial red brick building may have been extended over the years but on the whole has stayed largely unchanged).

Now follow the road SA uphill towards the town, (passing the golf club on your L). Finally you will reach a main road junction where you should TL for the short walk back to Earls Colne and the end of your walk.

Earls Colne station 1910 (P Johnson)

The station forecourt today (author)

St Andrews Church, Colne Engaine (author)

The Lion pub, Earls Colne (author)

Castle Hedingham

Distance: 5¾ miles
Map: OS Explorer 195 (GR 786354)

Getting there:
Castle Hedingham is off the A1017 between Halstead and Great Yeldham

Parking:
You can park with care in the town

Pubs on route:
The Bell Inn and Wheatsheaf in Castle Hedingham
The White Hart, Great Yeldham

Route Map

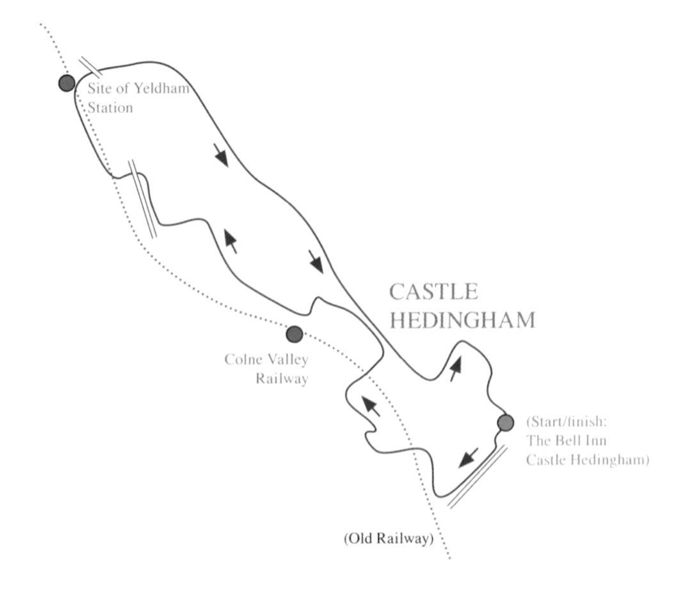

The Walk

A great walk starting in Castle Hedingham which ventures off along the Colne Valley to pass the preserved railway before picking up the old railway embankment near Yeldham to return to town via the Castle. If you wish to visit the Colne Valley Railway during your walk please check the opening hours:
www.colnevalleyrailway.co.uk
Tel: 01787 461174

Start on the High Street in Castle Hedingham outside the Bell Inn (opposite the Post Office). With the pub behind you TL and follow the main road ahead to pass the Wheatsheaf pub on Queen Street. Continue SA and follow the road as it leaves town. After a short walk you will cross the River Colne using a road bridge (a dismantled railway bridge lies just ahead). Immediately after the river TR at a FPS and follow the enclosed track ahead. On reaching a small wooded area continue SA following the hedge on the L and continue on this track as it bears round to the L. Cross over the old railway embankment to enter a field.

Now follow the RHFE to follow the river and carry on SA to reach a road. At the road immediately TR and cross the river at a bridge. After 50yds TL at FPS onto a good grass track and go SA across the field in front of you. (The Colne Valley Railway is now behind the hedge over to your R). Eventually the track bears to the R to reach a gate where you can cross the railway to reach another gate. Now proceed SA following the LHFE to finally reach a road (Kirby Hall Road).

TL onto the road and go SA for about 300yds to reach a FPS. TL and continue SA to follow a line of trees to reach the field corner. Cross a plank bridge and TL to follow the LHFE for a long walk with the railway over to your L. Pass under the high voltage cables and after another 500yds you should reach the field corner. TL through the hedge and go SA towards a farm (Poole Farm).

Just before the farm buildings TL onto a dirt track and pass some stables to reach a tarmac road. Finally TL to reach the main road ahead. Now TL and follow this busy road (A1017) for about 500yds to reach the entrance to the Colne Valley Railway (check in advance for opening times).

The Sible and Castle Hedingham station buildings are original. However, they have been moved some half a mile, brick by brick, from the station's original location in the town centre. The original site is now industrial premises. The railway museum has a large range of working locomotives as well as lots of assorted memorabilia. On leaving the railway go back to the main road and TR for 500yds to bring you back to the entrance to Poole Farm.

Stay on the main road and proceed SA following the footpath. Ignore the first FPS that you come to (after about 100yds) and continue SA, passing houses on the L and R. After 400yds look for a FPS on the L, (opposite a cottage) and TL to follow a grassy track. Keep to the L and go through several gates, the last of which will bring you to a black weather-boarded house. Pass the house on your R and cross the old (half-buried) brick railway bridge. Immediately TR and pass a horse jumping paddock on your L. Now continue SA on a good grass track to eventually head downhill to reach the old railway formation. TL and follow the enclosed track along the railway embankment. Cross the river using the small bridge on the L (sadly the old railway bridge has long gone) and continue SA on a good track towards the road ahead (railway should now be on your R).

At the road TR (the remains of Yeldham Station are directly on the L) and proceed SA to the road junction ahead. TR onto the main road and after 30yds TL at a FPS. (If you wish to visit the White Hart pub just stay on this road for another 100yds). Follow the track SA as it eventually heads uphill. At the top of the hill bear R to reach a gate and immediately TR to follow the footpath directly across the field ahead (don't follow the field edge).

Having crossed the field you will reach a FPS at the field edge. Go through the hedge and across the next field to reach a FPS at the field corner. Now go SA following the LHFE and at the next field corner go SA and follow the RHFE to reach a gate. Cross a small plank bridge, TL and go SA across the next field for about 300yds to reach a FPS. TL at FPS and after 50yds TR to follow a good grassy track uphill. Now continue along this track for a long walk to eventually follow the LHFE. Finally you will pass a high voltage pylon where you should TL to reach a FPS by a road.

TR onto the road and proceed SA to follow this quiet country lane as it heads back towards Hedingham. Eventually you will reach a school on the L. TL at FPS (just before the school) and follow the RHFE uphill to reach the field corner. TR at FPS and proceed SA following the LHFE. There are some good views of the Colne Valley from here.

At the bottom corner of the field go through the hedge to reach an enclosed track. Now TR and follow this footpath into town. On reaching a road TL and immediately TR down Crown Street. After 300yds bear L along Church Ponds to pass the church on your R. When you reach Falcon Square TR onto King Street and follow the road ahead to bring you back to the Bell Inn and the end of your walk.

Sible and Castle Hedingham station 1947 (Lens of Sutton)

Part of the track today at the Museum (author)

Wivenhoe to Brightlingsea

The Town of Brightlingsea with its important fishing and oyster industry was linked to Wivenhoe with a single-track railway in 1866. The five and a half mile branch line had no intermediate stations and used a swing-bridge to cross Arlesford Creek. The line itself followed the path of the River Colne as it exits into the Thames Estuary and was therefore a low lying structure. This proved to be problematic during the East Coast Floods of 1953 when several miles of track were washed away. However the line was rebuilt and by 1957 diesel engines had replaced steam.

Like many other branch lines Wivenhoe to Brightlingsea suffered from the rise in car and bus traffic and it was finally named for closure in the Beeching Report. Despite a spirited campaign from locals the last train ran in 1964. Today much of the old railway embankment is still accessible. In particular the stretch from Arlesford Creek to Brightlingsea is a great walk and must have made for a lovely railway journey in its heyday. Sadly the old Brightlingsea station building has long since been demolished. However, despite much of the swing-bridge being dismantled, its original supporting pillars are still present. Wivenhoe is still a working station.

Wivenhoe

Distance: 7 miles
Map: OS Explorer 184 (GR 036215)

Getting there:

Wivenhoe can be reached using the A133 and B1028 south of Colchester. The town is also on the mainline railway network from Liverpool Street.

Parking:

There is parking available at the railway station

Food and drink on route:

Pubs are The Station Hotel, The Black Buoy and The Rose and Crown in Wivenhoe. The Pointer in Alresford.

Route Map

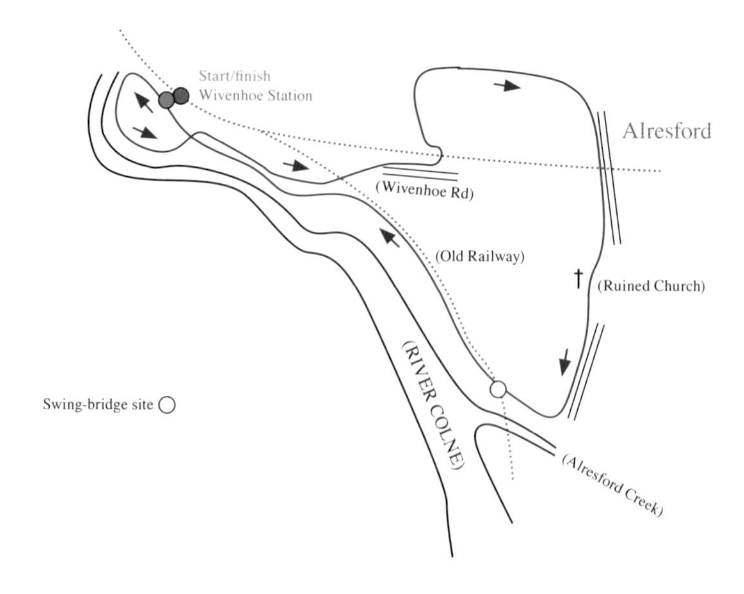

The Walk

A longer walk which starts at the railway station before taking a journey along the banks of the River Colne and crossing the old railway to visit Alresford; returning via the site of the old swing bridge at Alresford Creek, and a long walk along the track-bed. This walk passes no fewer than four local pubs.

Start at Wivenhoe railway station. With your back to the station TR and walk through the car park passing a wooden gate to reach the 'Wivenhoe Trail'. Don't follow the trail but keep right and follow the track beside the railway. After about 600yds TL at FPS along an enclosed track (the River Colne will be on your R) and follow this riverside path as it slowly curves around back towards Wivenhoe. On reaching some new-build houses TR down West Quay and follow the path beside river and pass the Sailing Club and British Legion. Now pass the Rose and Crown pub and after 100yds TL up a small road (Bethany Street) to reach the Black Buoy pub at East Street.

Now TR down Brook Street and follow this winding lane to reach the Wivenhoe Business Centre. At this road junction take the second right turn (with a red brick house on the corner) and go SA through new-build houses towards the river and the Colne Barrier. At the Colne Barrier follow the footpath ahead as it passes the Sailing Club and go SA following the riverbank. (The old railway was on the raised embankment to your L).

After 200yds TL down a set of steps (there may be no FPS here) and follow the grassy path to your R to reach the old railway. At a stile cross the railway and continue SA on a good track. At a gate follow the enclosed track SA uphill (look out for sheep!) and at the top of hill exit onto a road. TR and follow the road SA keeping to the left-hand verge and after passing two houses TL at FPS, go over a stile and head towards the existing railway line. Cross the railway (watching out for trains) and immediately TL along an enclosed track to enter a wood.

Pass the sand and gravel workings to reach a gravel road and go SA for 30yds to reach a gate on R. TR and follow the track through woods keeping to the left-hand path beside a brook on L. At the edge of wood cross stile to reach a dirt road. TR and go SA and as road bears L go SA on a good track towards another wood ahead. At FPS go SA into wood and follow the path to reach a road. Exit onto road (Cockaynes Lane) and TR to follow this quite lane into the village of Alresford.

At the next junction TR and continue through village to reach the station. Go over level crossing and proceed SA to next road junction. (The Pointer pub is on the right here). Go SA down Church Road to exit the village. Eventually you will reach the disused St Andrews Church on your R. Continue down Church Road to pass a gravel workings on your R and as road finally comes to an end (at Alresford Creek) TR at FPS and follow the track with Creek on your L. As you pass a house that lays back on the R you will see the old railway as it turns L ahead of you to cross the Creek using the now demolished swing bridge. (You can detour down to the crossing point where you will find the concrete pillars that held the bridge in place. The same can also be seen on the opposite bank of the creek). Now go back to the footpath, TL and proceed SA back towards Wivenhoe.

This part of the walk follows the old railway track-bed. After a considerable walk exit the enclosed track to follow the bank of the Colne. (The railway is now 20yds to your R and it follows this tree-lined route into town). Continue SA on this gravel track and pass the Sailing Club to reach the Colne Barrier. Go SA on the road (through new-build houses) to reach the Business Centre and TL up Brook Street, passing the Black Buoy pub on L to reach Rose Lane (Rose and Crown pub is down here). Don't go down Rose Lane but continue on the main road to reach its junction with the High Street. TR passing shops and take the first left turn up West Road. Finally go SA to bring you back to Wivenhoe station and the end of your walk.

Wivenhoe station in the 1930s (Lens of Sutton)

A very rare photo of the old swing-bridge (Brightlingsea Museum)

Site of the old swing-bridge (author)

The ruins of St Andrews Church, Alresford (author)

Brightlingsea

Distance: 6½ miles
Map: OS Explorer 184 (GR 084166)

Getting there:
Brightlingsea is on the B1029 which can be accessed from the A120.
Nearest railway station is Alresford.

Parking:
There should be plenty of on-street parking near the Station Tavern

Food and drink on route:
Various pubs and shops in the centre of Brightlingsea

Local Interest:
Brightlingsea Museum, 1 Duke Street, Brightlingsea.
Tel: 01206 303286

Route Map

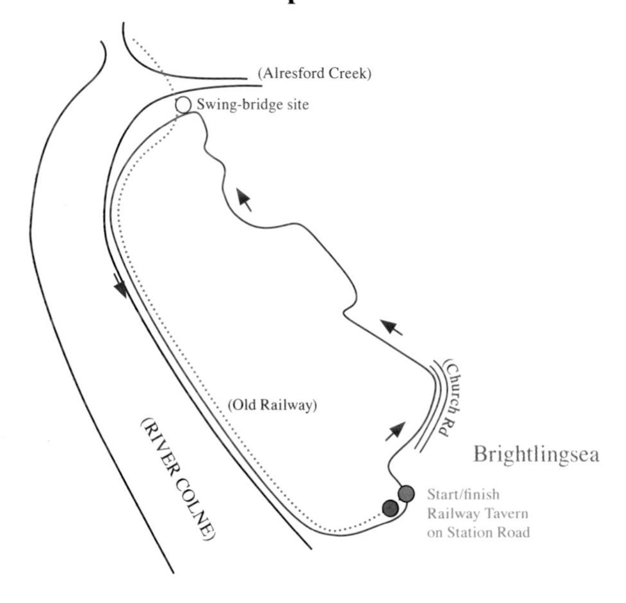

The Walk

Starting with a walk through the town before heading towards Alresford Creek and the old swing-bridge site and then a long walk following the old railway along the bank of River Colne to return to Brightlingsea. Try to get to the Museum if you can.

Start at the Railway Tavern on Station Road, (opposite the Community Centre). (If you wish to visit Brightlingsea Museum see end of chapter)*. With the pub behind you TR up Lower Park Road, pass the fire station and follow the road uphill until it bears to the L and becomes Church Road. Now continue SA, passing the Cherry Tree pub and the water tower on your L. Carry on this road as it passes a sports centre and school and after 500yds look for a FPS on L as the road turns to the R. Now TL onto a tarmac road and go SA past a playing field on your L. As the road turns L you should TR onto an enclosed track and continue SA to reach a quarry.

TR for 30yds and at a metal gate TL onto a good track. At the end of track cross over the dirt road onto an enclosed track SA, go down a set of steps and proceed across the next field, bearing slightly R. At field edge go up the hill in front of you to find a FPS by a road. TL and follow the right hand fork, eventually passing a house on R and continue SA following a good track downhill towards the River Colne.After a long walk you will reach Alresford Creek, TL at FPS, go through kissing gate and proceed SA along the riverbank (with the Creek on your R) towards the old swing bridge site. (You may wish to visit the remains of the bridge but this can only be done with care at low tide).

Now follow the track as it turns sharp L to follow the River Colne. You are now on the old track-bed and will stay on it for most of the remainder of this walk. This part of the Wivenhoe to Brightlingsea railway must have made for a beautiful journey with the Colne on the right and gently sloping hills on the left.

Now proceed SA for the long walk back to Brightlingsea. Eventually you will reach some beach huts beside the Bateman's Tower, follow the track as it goes behind the huts and bears L to pass a skateboard park on the R. As the track ends go down a set of steps and TL following a road to pass a swimming pool and boating lake on R. Finally, pass the Community Centre on L (this was the site of Brightlingsea station) and at the road junction go SA back into Station Road and the end of the walk.

* Brightlingsea Museum is at 1 Duke Street, Brightlingsea. It is 300yds back up Station Road. It has a very interesting section on the old railway including a scale model of the old Brightlingsea Station.

The museum is open from Easter to the last weekend in September:
Saturdays 10am - 4pm
Sundays 2 – 5pm
Mondays 2 – 5pm
Please call ahead to check times: 01206 303286

Looking across Alresford Creek today (author)

Brightlingsea station in the 1950s (NRM Collection)

Following the track-bed away from the swingbridge site (author)

Mangapps Railway Museum

The Mangapps Museum is unique among the other preserved railways in Essex in that it has been created from nothing. There never was a railway here. Every train, piece of track, signal box and carriage has been brought here by the Jolly family and their enthusiastic band of supporters to create a ¾ mile working railway. Along with steam and diesel engines you will find several recreated signal boxes, platforms and waiting rooms and probably the largest collection of signalling equipment in the UK. Several static carriages have been converted into small museums and there is even an old London Underground Tube train on site. In addition to this Mangapps has a very large collection of smaller railway relics such as old station posters, station nameplates and staff uniforms. Check the Mangapps website for their opening hours.

www.mangapps.co.uk
Tel: 01621 784898

Burnham to Mangapps

Distance: 4 miles
Map: OS Explorer 176 (GR 952955)

Getting there:

Burnham-on-Crouch is at the end of the B1021 about 9 miles east of South Woodham Ferrers and the A130 dual carriageway. It is also on the mainline railway from Liverpool Street

Parking:

There are several car parks in the town plus some on-street parking

Pubs on route:

The Victoria Inn, White Harte Hotel, Ship Inn and Star Inn are all in Burnham

Route Map

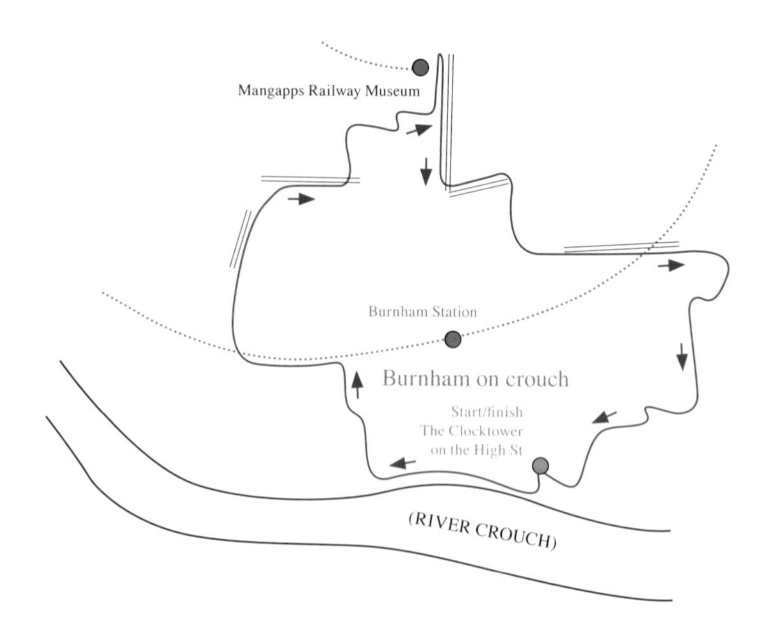

The Walk

The only walk in the book not to follow a lost branch line. Instead we start and finish in Burnham on Crouch and walk via the waterfront to Mangapps Museum before returning to town passing no fewer than four local pubs.

For Mangapps Railway Museum opening hours:
Tel: 01621 784898
Web: www.mangapps.co.uk

Start at the Clocktower in Burnham High Street. With the clock behind you TL and almost immediately TL again down Shore Road to bring you to the river. TR along to waterfront to pass the White Harte Hotel and the Star Inn and follow this riverside walkway through the town until you eventually pass Riverside Park on your R. Continue SA along the path towards the Marina ahead. On reaching the Marina TR and follow the path with the moorings on your L until you get to the back of the boatyard. Now look for a large bar and restaurant (the Swallowtail) and TR to walk up the Marina approach road. Follow this road slightly uphill until you reach a FPS just before the railway.

TL and follow this footpath SA with the railway on your R and the river down to your L. Continue until you reach a FPS beside a railway crossing. Now TR, cross the track and follow the footpath SA. Cross into the next field and follow the LHFE towards a house ahead. On reaching a road TR and continue SA until you reach a main road junction. Proceed SA across the road (to a FPS) and follow the track ahead between houses to eventually bring you to a small lane. TR onto the lane and go SA for about 500yds to reach a FPS by a cottage. TL and follow the grass track SA to pass a small pond on your R. Go SA across the next field (Mangapps is ahead of you). On reaching the field edge TR and follow the LHFE for 200yds, then TL into the next field, (the FPS may be missing here). At this junction of several fields immediately TR and follow the RHFE to pass behind some houses.

When you reach the field corner TR and follow the track beside a house for 200yds to bring you to a dirt road. TL onto the road for 50yds and just before Mangapps Farm TR at a FPS to follow an enclosed track to reach a main road. TL onto the road (stay on the LH verge where possible) and go SA for 300yds to reach the entrance to Mangapps Museum.

When you leave the Museum retrace your steps along the gravel driveway to bring you back to the main road. Now TR and follow the verge for 200yds until the footpath begins. Follow this road SA as you come into the outskirts of Burnham, passing several small turnings as you do so. Eventually you will come to a bend in the road (Eves Corner) where you should TL down Mill Road (marked as a dead-end). Go SA down the road for about 500yds and where the road bends sharply L look for a FPS and follow the dirt track ahead towards Romans Farm. Pass the farmhouse on your L and cross a small brook at a wooden bridge. Now continue SA on a dirt track as you head uphill towards some houses.

On reaching a road TL and go SA to follow this lane as you cross the railway at a road bridge. Carry on SA for a long walk to pass first Brook Farm on your L and then a small row of houses. About 200yds further along you will come to a FPS. TR and pass between farm buildings to follow a concrete path SA. At the end of a row of trees TR at the FPS and follow the RHFE for 200yds to reach another FPS. Now turn sh arp L and follow the track across the field. On reaching a hedge go SA into the next field to follow a row of trees ahead. Ignore the first FPS that you come to (pointing L) and about 100yds further along look for another FPS (pointing R). TR at this field corner and follow the LHFE until the track bears L towards a road. On reaching the road TR and follow this winding road as it brings you into Burnham. Ignore the first few minor roads and eventually you will reach Silver Road. Now TL and follow Silver Road SA to pass first the Victoria Inn and then the Ship Inn as you arrive back to the High Street and the Clocktower at the end of your walk.

Mangapps main entrance. Please check ahead for opening times (author)

The railway sidings have all been created on a greenfield site (author)

The Museum has an amazing display of railway signalling and signage (author)

The Victoria Inn, Burnham (author)

Something Found

I hope that in having walked the lost railways in this book you have been able to understand how and why they came to these far flung places. But it is also worth exploring the reasons why they declined and ultimately what kind of county has been left behind with their loss. What is clear is that there was no one single cause of the decline of branch-line Britain but rather that several events conspired over time to make their closure inevitable. So let's explore those reasons, and then take a look at Essex today and ask ourselves what kind of county remains.

Firstly, who or what is to blame for the loss of these branch lines? Well, there are several factors that all contributed to the decline of the railways and they all have their part to play. To begin with the entire system (or lack of one) that allowed all these different railway companies, big and small to spring up across the country but never as part of a larger overall plan, was bound to create inefficiencies. Although this free-for-all left us with the variety of lines that can be walked in this book it also led to many lines never really making a profit or carrying a great number of passengers throughout their lives. So it is ironic that by the nature of the way that the railways grew in the 1900s it was also to contribute to their downfall.

The grouping of the railways in 1923 was undoubtedly a good idea and at least meant that for the first time all the Essex lines all came under the central control of the LNER. However, with the end of the Second World War came two big problems: the need to modernise the railways and the rise of the motorcar. Let's take the Modernisation Plan of 1955. In theory this was a great idea but in practice it became a mess. The plan to spend £1.5 billion on replacing steam with diesel and electric was poorly managed with confused objectives.

With the commissioning of new rolling stock poorly implemented and often prone to break down, the good money that should have been spent on new, modern services was frittered away on what was probably the last chance to really make the system work. Furthermore, the rise in popularity of the motorcar was to go from strength to strength with construction of the first motorways and the gradual move towards transporting goods by lorry rather than rail.

All of this left British Railways with the big problem of its costs growing while its revenue fell. Into the picture now comes Dr Richard Beeching who, doing the Conservative Government's bidding, came up with his now infamous report. His central premise, that the branch lines would never make money and instead investment should be focused on the mainline stations, had one fatal flaw: his suggestion that travellers would now drive or get bussed to their nearest mainline station, didn't actually happen. On the whole once in their cars, people stayed in them, often bypassing the railway completely. But Beeching did have a point; particularly when his report noted that for many branch lines to make a profit they would have to carry up to four times the current passenger numbers plus quadruple the average ticket price. Clearly this was just not possible and led the way for the axe to fall. Despite all the uproar at the time railway closures actually continued long after Beeching, through both Labour and Conservative Governments until the late 1970s.

So, take your pick: was it the disorganised way the railways grew up, the botched Modernisation Plan, the Beeching axe, or the rise of the motor car? The answer, of course, is that they all played their part. But probably the crucial downfall was the Modernisation Plan. Here was a chance to get things right. If the national government and the management of British Railways had really thought through the plan, transformed the outdated working practices, perhaps closed the worst performing branch lines and brought the unions on board, who knows, we could be looking at a very different railway today.

The last chance to save branch-line Britain had been wasted. Perhaps the greatest irony of all is that the country that invented the railway seems to have had the most trouble actually making it work.

Let's turn to how Essex has fared since the demise of these branch lines. Although the loss of a line cannot be seen as a good thing to towns such as Halstead or Great Dunmow, it should not be seen as sounding the death-knell either. For towns and communities do not collapse with the removal of a railway, they just grow at a slower pace. As we may expect the towns with the greatest growth are those with a continuing railway presence (Witham, Braintree) but surprisingly those that have lost out do not collapse or even wither. In fact how often do you hear the complaint that many towns are now just too large, whereas to judge them by their populations both Halstead and Dunmow have continued to grow, but at a more manageable level. It seems as if the loss of a railway acts as a regulator on never-ending expansion of many urban areas: house prices come down, commuters find them less attractive, only to become attractive in a different way. Indeed some of the most beautiful and rural parts of the county are very close to former branch lines: Earls Colne, Ashdon, Blake Hall, Thaxted, Tollesbury, the list goes on. Would these areas still be as charming and unspoilt today if the railways were still present? Probably not.

Our railway heritage is still out there to be rediscovered. Sometimes it is easy to spot, sometimes not. Occasionally former lines will be put to good use, as with The Flitch Way, or one of the several preserved railways that are kept going by groups of dedicated enthusiasts and hardy visitors. But more often than not they have been left for nature to slowly reclaim these wonderful places. These embankments, buildings and hedgerows are teeming with wildlife but more than that they hark back to an era of great innovation and promise. The fact that this promise has not always been realised does not mean failure, for we have been left with something very precious and very English. Essex today is more beautiful and revealing because of something we gained and then foolishly lost.

L
N
E

Lines not in this Book

There are two branch lines that do not appear in this book. They are the Corringham Light Railway, and the Mistley Thorpe and Walton Railway. They have not been included as there is insufficient railway structure left remaining to warrant any walks.

As with other Light Railways the Corringham Light Railway (running from Corringham to Coryton) was built to a lesser standard than the more traditional lines and has now been virtually eliminated. The remaining trackbed that is still present can be found at Corringham station using an OS map (GR 713838). There may also be some platform remaining at Coryton. For further reading there is a very useful book called The Corringham Light Railway, written by Peter Kay.

The Mistley Thorpe and Walton Railway was abandoned during construction and never saw any train service at all. OS map number 184 still shows some of the remaining track-bed at GR 130310 and a bridge at GR 131314.

Further Reading

Most Branch Lines have had books written about them at one time or another and a good way to find them is to visit your local bookshop where it is often possible to get hold of these rare and possibly out of print publications. There are also various books and websites where you can follow up the details of the Branch Lines discussed in this book.

Website:

www.disused-stations.org.uk

Books:

Railway Posters 1923-1947
by Beverley Cole and Richard Durack

A Historical Dictionary of Railways in the British Isles
by David Wragg

Essex Railway Heritage
by Peter Kay